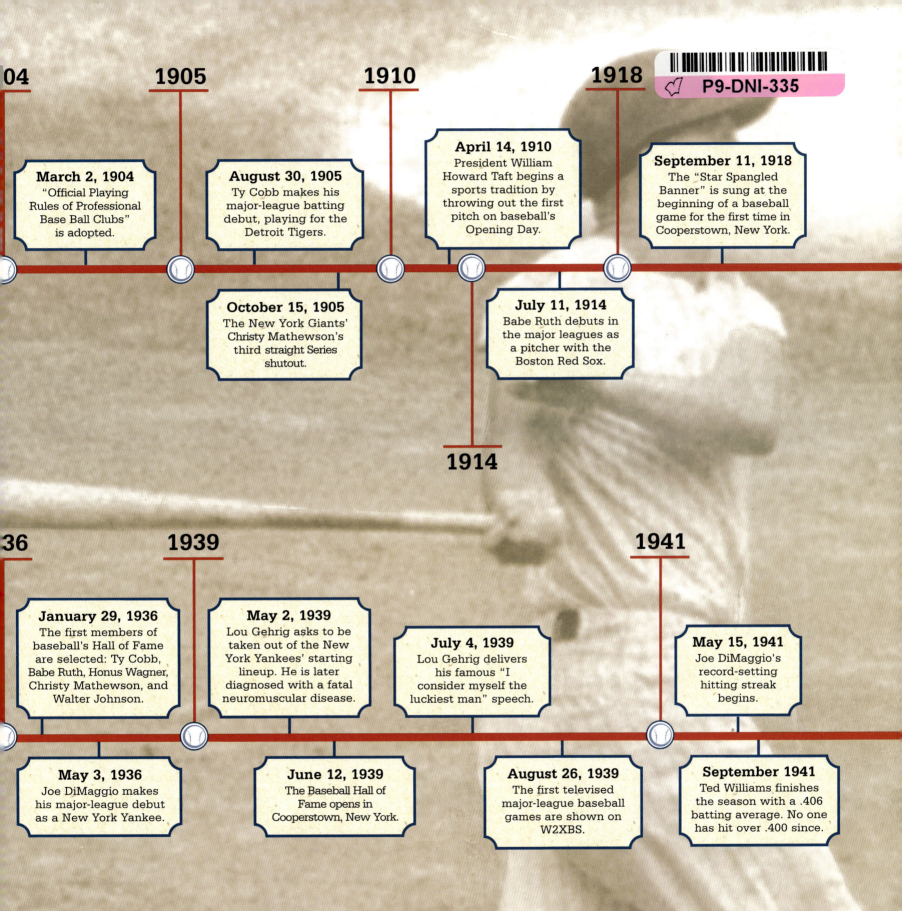

**04**

**1905**

**1910**

**1918**

**March 2, 1904**
"Official Playing Rules of Professional Base Ball Clubs" is adopted.

**August 30, 1905**
Ty Cobb makes his major-league batting debut, playing for the Detroit Tigers.

**April 14, 1910**
President William Howard Taft begins a sports tradition by throwing out the first pitch on baseball's Opening Day.

**September 11, 1918**
The "Star Spangled Banner" is sung at the beginning of a baseball game for the first time in Cooperstown, New York.

**October 15, 1905**
The New York Giants' Christy Mathewson's third straight Series shutout.

**July 11, 1914**
Babe Ruth debuts in the major leagues as a pitcher with the Boston Red Sox.

**1914**

**36**

**1939**

**1941**

**January 29, 1936**
The first members of baseball's Hall of Fame are selected: Ty Cobb, Babe Ruth, Honus Wagner, Christy Mathewson, and Walter Johnson.

**May 2, 1939**
Lou Gehrig asks to be taken out of the New York Yankees' starting lineup. He is later diagnosed with a fatal neuromuscular disease.

**July 4, 1939**
Lou Gehrig delivers his famous "I consider myself the luckiest man" speech.

**May 15, 1941**
Joe DiMaggio's record-setting hitting streak begins.

**May 3, 1936**
Joe DiMaggio makes his major-league debut as a New York Yankee.

**June 12, 1939**
The Baseball Hall of Fame opens in Cooperstown, New York.

**August 26, 1939**
The first televised major-league baseball games are shown on W2XBS.

**September 1941**
Ted Williams finishes the season with a .406 batting average. No one has hit over .400 since.

# HEROES
## of BASEBALL

robert
lipsyte

The Men Who Made It America's Favorite Game

A Byron Preiss Visual Publications, Inc., Book
**ATHENEUM BOOKS FOR YOUNG READERS**
NEW YORK  LONDON  TORONTO  SYDNEY

For Alfred Major Lipsyte,
Rookie of the Year

ACKNOWLEDGMENTS
This was a team effort, just like baseball. There was Roger Cooper, super scout and general manager, who put the writing and editing team together and told us we could win. Caitlyn Dlouhy, our field manager, made the final decisions from the dugout. Even though we argued with the skipper, her decisions were the right ones. The coach who told us when to hit, when to run and when to rewrite was Howard (Commander) Zimmerman. Could the Mets use him! Finally, I never would have finished the ninth inning without my friend and battery-mate, the historian Peter Levine, who blocked wild pitches and nailed runners trying to steal.

PHOTO CREDITS
The following photographs are courtesy of the National Baseball Hall of Fame Library, Cooperstown, New York: title page, table of contents, pages 6, 7, 8, 9, 11, 12, 17, 19, 21, 23, 24, 25, 26, 28, 34, 35, 36, 38, 39, 42, 47, 52, 54, 55, 65, 68 *(top and bottom)*, 75, 76, 82, 84, 87, 88 *(top left, top right, and bottom right)*, 92 *(bottom)*

The following photographs are copyright © AP Wide World Photo: pages 10, 20, 31, 33, 41, 43, 45, 46, 48 *(top and bottom)*, 49, 51, 53, 55, 56, 57, 58, 61, 63, 64, 66, 67, 69, 71 *(left and right)*, 72, 73, 74, 77 *(top and bottom)*, 79, 80, 81, 83, 84 *(bottom)*, 85, 86, 88 *(bottom left)*, 89, 90, 91, 92 *(top)*, 93 *(top and bottom right)*

The photograph on page 5 is courtesy of the author.

*Title page caption*: One of the greatest pitchers of all time, Satchel Paige
*Table of contents caption*: Babe Ruth in the batter's box.

Atheneum Books for Young Readers • An imprint of Simon & Schuster Children's Publishing Division • 1230 Avenue of the Americas, New York, New York 10020 • Text copyright © 2006 by Robert Lipsyte • All rights reserved, including the right of reproduction in whole or in part in any form. • Book design by Edie Weinberg • The text for this book is set in Serifa. • Manufactured in the United States of America • 10 9 8 7 6 5 4 3 2 • Library of Congress Cataloging-in-Publication Data • Lipsyte, Robert. • Heroes of baseball: the men who made it America's favorite game / Robert Lipsyte. • p. cm. • ISBN-13: 978-0-689-86741-5 • ISBN-10: 0-689-86741-7 • 1. Baseball players—United States—Biography. 2. Baseball—United States—History. I. Title. • GV863.A1L56 2006 • 796.357'092'2'—dc22 • 2005010841

# CONTENTS

# Introduction
# Play Ball!

**M**y first big assignment as a young sportswriter for *The New York Times* was to cover the spring training of a brand-new major league team called the New York Mets. This was in 1962. The Mets were an expansion team, which meant that their first roster was mostly made up of players the other teams were willing to give up, older guys, rookies, and players who had never quite made it. The word was that the Mets were going to be very, very bad.

So I brought my glove along to spring training.

That sounds pretty crazy now, especially to me. I wasn't even that great a baseball player. But because it's a game that most Americans have played, or at least watched, it seems to belong to us in special ways. I would never dream of bringing my helmet to a pro-football training camp or my ice skates to a hockey workout (maybe if I was Canadian, I might). But I brought my glove and even had a little fantasy about my last story for the paper, which would begin, "Robert 'Bobo' Lipsyte, a former reporter for this newspaper, signed a contract with the New York Mets today and was assigned to the club's Class A minor-league team, where he will play second base.

'Can't wait for him to make it to the big club,' said Mets Manager Casey Stengel. 'Only hope he remembers not to take notes in the field.'"

I ended up using the glove a few times, shagging balls in the outfield. I even got up to the plate against a coach throwing batting practice. It was a great learning experience. Catching a major league line drive feels like catching a bullet. And I never came close to making contact with those soft pitches down the middle. By the time I was ready to swing, they were thudding into the catcher's mitt.

Those Mets turned out to be bad all right—they posted some of the worst statistics in baseball history—but I came to appreciate how truly wondrous the skills of major-league players are, even the ones who aren't stars, who barely make the team. They may be playing a child's game, but they certainly are not playing it childishly.

People who think that baseball is the best game—and I am one of them—have different reasons for thinking so. And I think all the reasons are right.

Some people think baseball is the best game, because it requires such special skills—hitting a little white ball hurtling along at 95 miles an hour with a skinny round stick, pitching that ball to a particular place in space while making it dip or rise or curve, throwing precisely to the right base while a runner slides into you, sprinting after a towering fly ball to make the catch that will save the game, knowing you may crash into the center field wall. Just watching players do these things makes our hearts pound!

Some people think that baseball is the best game because it is so elegant. The beautiful geometry of the field, the precision of the distances between bases, the wonderful journey from home all the way back home seems like a tale of adventure. It is a tale with excitement and danger, but none of the extreme violence of football and hockey or the in-your-face machismo of basketball. The winners are cool. And patient. A game is timeless—there's no whistle at the end. Theoretically a game can go on forever, so long as you don't make the last out.

Some people think that baseball is the best game, because its history is so rich with interesting characters—the heroes of the game. That's what this book is about. There have been hundreds of fascinating people among the thousands who have played major-league ball. I've had to concentrate on a few I thought made the most impact by bringing the game to vivid life in their own times and contributing in important, historical ways to

*Above*: Author Robert "Bobo" Lipsyte with one of his baseball heroes, Joe DiMaggio.

Some of our heroes of the game were also great human beings. Jackie Robinson and Curt Flood were heroes who stood up for their principles and not only made baseball a better game, but America a better place. Some of them had tremendous positive impact on others. Babe Ruth, a throwaway kid, was an enormous inspiration to an America of struggling immigrants. Mickey Mantle played hard despite a painful bone disease in his legs, and as he was dying in 1995, became an eloquent spokesman for organ donation.

Of course, not all the great players were great people. Some were ordinary guys with extraordinary talents, and some had human flaws that disappointed us. Pete Rose gambled on his own games, which made fans wonder about the honesty of those games, and a number of players have used illegal drugs to enhance their skills, which is unfair to those who want to play clean.

And then there was Ty Cobb, a vicious, loud-mouthed bully. Hardly anyone liked him. Even his own teammates kept their distance, afraid he'd explode, scream at them, even punch them out. So how could he be one of my heroes of baseball?

It would be terrific if all the athletes we cheered for were good guys, the role models who are supposed to be our shining examples. But like scientists, authors, elected officials, and military leaders who have impact on our daily lives, not all athletes are

make it the game we now know and love.

As you will read in this book, baseball didn't just happen by accident. One of the greatest of its early players, a pitcher named Albert G. Spalding, set out to make himself rich by making the game America's National Pastime. He claimed that the game had such positive values, it would make people better.

*Above:* Ty Cobb was the perfect player for his time.

as praiseworthy in their personal lives as they are in their work.

And baseball is work, and the players we admire are those who bring to their work the willingness to play hard, help their team win, and give us pleasure watching them. Those who become our heroes go beyond that. Some are the players who, with skill and intensity, show us how the game was made to be played (like Ty Cobb). And some show us, through their play, the values of teamwork, courage, and honor (like Hank Aaron). Some, through their personalities and style, help define the age in which they lived (Babe Ruth). A very few, through their courage and personal sacrifice, give us a glimpse of the potential for heroism that every one of us, with or without a mitt, is born with (Jackie Robinson).

Thanks to ESPN and wall-to-wall sports TV, the current crop of baseball heroes seems to hang out in our living rooms. We feel we really know Mark McGwire, Sammy Sosa, Barry Bonds, A-Rod, Roger Clemens, Cal Ripken Jr., Ken Griffey Jr., and Derek Jeter.

After you read this book, I hope you'll also feel you know some of the older heroes of baseball who brought our game to life and kept it alive for us.

*Above:* Babe Ruth doing what he did best—whacking another home run.

# ① Big Al Leads Off

**P**icture yourself on a hot summer day in a new town far from all your friends. You don't know anyone. You're a stranger in a strange place. You feel shy and lonely. Your parents tell you that everything will work out fine. But you're not so sure. You worry about how you will fit in and make new friends.

You sit on a hill overlooking a field where kids your age are playing baseball. You wish you could join them, but no one seems to notice you. You watch a few innings and then decide to leave. Tears burn your eyes.

Then, suddenly, the batter hits a long fly over the center fielder's head. It comes straight toward you. Without thinking, you leap up and snatch it out of the air with your bare hand. You fire a clothesline peg to the shortstop, who tags

out the runner trying to scoot back to second base.

Everyone stops and stares at you. They begin to run toward you, yelling. At first you think they're angry at you for disrupting their game. You turn to run away. But they just want to congratulate you on your great catch and mighty throw. They want you to join their game.

They want to be friends.

You realize that everything will be all right. You're going to like this new town—thanks to baseball.

Sound a little fantastic? Maybe. But that's just the kind of story that Albert G. Spalding, the man behind baseball, liked to tell about himself and about how baseball could help you get the most out of life.

A. G. Spalding, also known as "Big Al," was baseball's first great pitcher. He was

*Opposite:* Elysian Fields in Hoboken, New Jersey, the site of the first official baseball game between two clubs on June 19, 1846.
*Above:* Portrait of A. G. Spalding after he had retired as a player.

## Baseball Cards

Honus Wagner card

Baseball cards have been around since the earliest days of professional baseball. The first card had a brown-tinted photograph of the 1869 Cincinnati Red Stockings on one side, and the team roster with blank space on the other side. Local businessmen would buy the cards, print their own ads on the back, and give them away to customers.

In 1887 a cigarette manufacturer, Goodwin & Company, offered a small, full-color card with each package of cigarettes it sold. These were the first cards sold nationwide. In 1914 and 1915, kids could even find cards in boxes of Cracker Jack.

The Goudey Gum Company started to include cards in their packages of gum in 1933. One penny bought you three pieces of bubble gum and a single baseball card. In 1948 the Bowman Card Company became the

also a visionary and a businessman. He set out to make baseball more than just a game. You can see how well he succeeded. Thanks to him baseball became known as America's National Pastime. He's a hero, because more than any other single person, A. G. made baseball—both as business and as sport—the game we know today. He was the founding father.

Young Albert grew up in the 1850s in Rockford, Illinois, a small city not far from Chicago. His father died when he was only eight years old. But then, baseball "discovered" him. By the time he was fifteen, he was the best pitcher in town. Often he would ditch high school to pitch for Forest City, the hometown team.

Forest City belonged to the National League of Base Ball Players. The league had begun as a group of amateur clubs. Originally its players were middle-class white men who played for fun and enjoyment. By the time Spalding came along in 1865, right after the Civil War, winning had become so important that teams often paid players or found them jobs that allowed them the time to play. Even back then, a winning baseball team could be a profitable investment as well as a way of promoting a city.

But A. G. had his eye on the big leagues. In 1871 he quit Forest City and joined the Boston Red Stockings, one of nine teams in baseball's first professional league, the National Association of Professional Base Ball Players (NAPBBP). By then he was better known as "Big Al." At 6'1" tall and almost 180 pounds, he was one of the largest men playing pro ball. As the best pitcher in the new league, he earned one of the highest salaries—$1,500 a year. (In those days, the average salary of a workingman in the United States was less than $500 a year.)

A. G. was worth every cent. He became professional baseball's first 200-game winner, earning most of those victories with the Boston club. He led the Red Stockings to the league championship four times.

When the NAPBBP began, the league fielded teams in large cities like Boston, New York, Philadelphia, and Chicago, and small cities like Fort Wayne, Indiana, and Troy, New York. The small cities often had trouble attracting enough fans to support the teams. Sometimes owners couldn't afford to pay their players. Scheduled games were cancelled without notice. Players jumped from team to team. Can you imagine a Chicago Cub just showing up one day to play as a Boston Red Sox? The NAPBBP was a shaky league.

In 1875, William Hulbert, a Chicago coal baron who owned the Chicago White Stockings, convinced A. G. to join his team and help establish a new league called the National League of Professional Baseball Clubs that would be financially stable. That was the start of the present National League.

Hulbert was a successful businessman, who went into baseball to make more money. His plan for the new National League avoided the problems of the old league. Teams were allowed only in cities with populations of at least 75,000 people. That way, he hoped to guarantee an audience. If teams didn't play all their

first to issue a baseball card set that they sold nationally. Topps became their main competition, and by 1955 stood alone. Today, Upper Deck, Pinnacle, and many other companies also make cards. None comes with gum.

There was a time when baseball cards were just fun to collect. They reminded you of how much you loved the game. One side of the cardboard card usually had a player's full-color autographed picture. The other side contained information about his baseball career.

In recent years, however, like baseball itself, producing and collecting cards has become a big business. In 1992, the combined sales for all card companies totaled $922 million. In that same year, former New York Yankee slugger Reggie Jackson signed his own contract with Upper Deck for $500,000, which allowed them to use his picture on their cards.

Collectors have sent the prices for old cards soaring. One 1909 Honus Wagner card, for instance, was sold for as high as $450,000!

Hall of Famers pose with their cards.

games or pay their players, they had to answer to the league, which acted as a government.

In 1876 Hulbert expelled the Philadelphia Athletics and the New York Mutuals from his league for failure to complete scheduled road trips. A year later, he banished four Louisville players for betting on games. And in 1878, the league established the reserve rule: From then on, a player no longer had the freedom to play for the team of his choice. He was bound to the club with which he had originally signed. The club had the sole power to play him or trade him to another club.

When A. G. first joined the Chicago White Stockings, he did more than just pitch, Hulbert named him captain and manager. A. G. retired as a player in 1877, and when Hulbert died in 1882, Spalding became the team's president and principal owner.

The White Stockings dominated the National League in the 1880s. They won five pennants in that decade and never finished worse than fifth place. Star players like Cap Anson became local heroes and role models. The *Chicago Tribune* noted that

small boys were encouraged to imitate the Chicago stars, much as they had been taught to be like George Washington!

Spalding became the guiding force behind professional baseball in the 1880s and early 1890s. Baseball was not a business on the same scale as the oil or steel industries, but, like other powerful capitalists of his time, such as Andrew Carnegie and John D. Rockefeller, A. G. worked hard to control his workers and create stable markets. He made his players sign a pledge that they would not drink alcohol during the season. Once, he even hired private detectives to follow Mike "King" Kelly, one of the game's early stars who played for the Louisville Colonels. The King was known to drink too much for his own good.

When the detectives reported to Spalding that they had seen Kelly drinking lemonade at 3 a.m., the King denied it. "It was straight whiskey," he told his boss. "I never drank a lemonade at that hour of the night."

Spalding eventually traded Kelly to Boston. He also vigorously enforced the reserve rule and fought tooth and nail with

*Above*: This nineteenth-century illustration shows that the ball was originally pitched underhand and there was no pitcher's mound.

players who sought to break free. During the 1891 season, he successfully blocked a number of established National League players from joining a new league started by other baseball players. He negotiated agreements with the rival American Association, which led to an interleague championship series, a forerunner of the World Series.

Through it all A. G. remained a vigorous, flamboyant character and always a shrewd businessman. Baseball was always more than a game for him. Not only did he believe that it turned young boys into strong, confident men, it was good business too, both on and off the field. On his desk, he kept this personal motto: "Anything is possible to him who dares." He lived by that motto. It was instrumental in helping him build the first great sporting-goods empire in the United States.

Long before there was Nike, Adidas, or Reebok, there was A. G. Spalding and Brothers. In 1876, with his brother, Walter, he opened the company's first sporting-goods store in Chicago. Within a decade, it dominated a new and growing industry, with factories and showrooms across America. The Spalding trademark became the symbol of quality on bats, baseballs, and bicycles. It remained so, well into the twentieth century.

Even as A. G. encouraged people to play sports, watch major-league baseball, and enjoy themselves, he understood that for many Americans, leisure time was still a new idea. For most people in post–Civil War America, daily life was basically a struggle for survival. People worked hard. In midwestern and eastern cities, new technology created factories that needed millions of workers. Although this brought prosperity to many in the middle class, immigrant laborers and American workingmen struggled to make ends meet. More than five million African Americans, once slaves and now free, battled to survive in a segregated land that still used violence to keep them second-class citizens. Out West, Americans were settling the frontier, sometimes killing Native Americans, who had been there first and didn't want to move away.

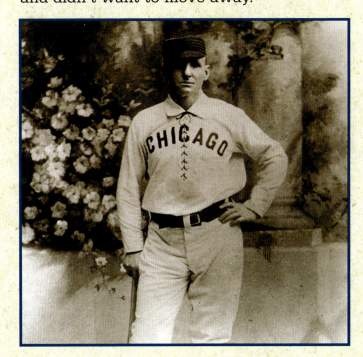

*Above:* Cap Anson, star player for the Chicago White Stockings, in the 1880s.

A. G. understood that in such a hard-working country, baseball needed to be promoted as more than just a game that was fun to watch or to play. Fun wasn't enough. The game had to have some positive value. So Spalding sold baseball as a uniquely American game that would build strong, loyal Americans. It would build character in boys. It would teach young men the discipline, teamwork, and responsibility they would need for work or war.

Spalding was well aware that forms of baseball had been played on American soil since the 1600s. English games like stoole ball and rounders were early versions of baseball. So was cricket. Nevertheless he declared baseball to be an American invention. Although he knew it wasn't true, he even established a national commission to prove that Abner Doubleday, a former Civil War general, had invented baseball in Cooperstown, New York, in 1839.

Spalding believed that his fabrication was for a good cause. He wanted to give his game that "Made in America" stamp, because baseball fostered what he considered American values. It was "the exponent of American Courage, Confidence, Combativeness; American Dash, Discipline, Determination; American Energy, Eagerness, Enthusiasm; American Pluck, Persistency, Performance," and so on.

Baseball, he insisted, had something for everyone. A. G. learned the game in a small town. Some people still thought of it as a rural sport for country boys. But Spalding helped promote it as a city game that would teach new Irish, Italian, and Jewish immigrants how to be Americans.

He even argued that watching it or playing it would relieve nervous tension among American middle-class men who were working so hard to build a great nation. Baseball was better than taking a drink or a nap!

Baseball, he declared, is "a man and soul builder. The genius of our institutions is democratic, and baseball is a democratic game."

But the truth was that

*Above:* The starting nine for the Cincinnati Red Stockings in 1869.

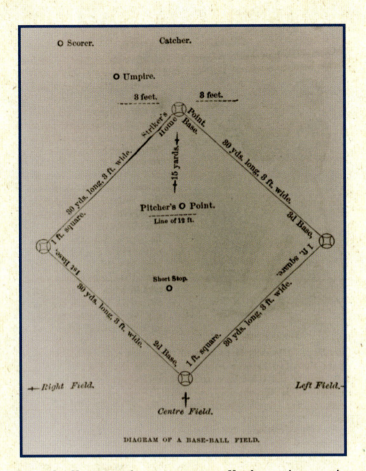

O Scorer.  Catcher.

O Umpire.

3 feet.  3 feet.

Striker's Point
Home Base.

80 yds. long, 3 ft. wide.
15 yards.

Pitcher's O Point.
Line of 12 ft.

3d Base.

1 ft. square.

1st Base.
1 ft. square.

Short Stop.
O

80 yds. long, 3 ft. wide.

80 yds. long, 3 ft. wide.
2d Base.
1 ft. square.

←Right Field.  Left Field.→

Centre Field.

DIAGRAM OF A BASE-BALL FIELD.

players and fans would turn away from the game if African Americans played, and thus hurt business? (Our heroes *do* have their flaws.)

"Now there's three things you can do in a baseball game. You can win or you can lose or it can rain."
—Casey Stengel, Dodger outfielder and Yankee manager

In any case a separate baseball world, the Negro Leagues, was eventually created. It was not until 1947, when Jackie Robinson took the field for the Brooklyn Dodgers, that blacks returned to the major leagues.

Once baseball was thriving in America, A. G. took his Chicago White Stockings and a hand-picked team of other professional players known as the All-Americans on an around-the-world tour.

When the Americans returned home after six months, they were greeted as conquering heroes. Mark Twain, author of *Huckleberry Finn* and one of America's greatest writers, toasted Spalding for introducing baseball—"the very symbol, the outward and visible expression of the drive

baseball wasn't open to all Americans in those days. Black Americans had played in the very early days of the game, but thanks to A. G. and Cap Anson, who took over as captain of the White Stockings when Spalding retired, they were barred from participating in the late 1880s. A. G. and Anson refused to let the White Stockings play against teams that fielded blacks, and they were powerful enough to get away with that. We don't know exactly why. Were they racists? Were they afraid that Southern

*Above:* Diagram of a baseball field in the 1880s. Note that the pitcher was 15 feet closer to the batter.

original team, stayed essentially the same throughout most of the twentieth century.

It seems fitting that the game's first hero was both a great player and a great businessman, a pitcher and a pitchman. The game that he made into America's National Pastime was a game we could be proud of, a game that, when played with spirit and ethics, reflected the best of American values. Without A. G. we wouldn't be cheering for the heroes who entertain and inspire us today. He was the daddy of all the heroes of baseball to come.

and push and rush and struggle of the raging, tearing, booming nineteenth century"—to the world.

Old A. G. was mighty pleased with himself. He truly believed that within baseball were the unique American virtues he hoped to spread throughout the world. And while he was making the rest of the world as good as America, he would also be selling it the bats and balls that his sporting-goods company manufactured.

A. G. died in 1915 at the age of sixty-five. By then, baseball was well established as the only real national professional sport in the United States. It was also big business, setting the stage for its expansion over the next nine decades. The organization and rules that were in place then, particularly the reserve rule that bound a player to his

*Above*: Abner Doubleday, the mythic father of American baseball. *Above, right*: Mike "King" Kelly of the Boston Beaneaters was the Babe Ruth of the 1880s. *Opposite*: When A. G. Spalding took an all-star team on a world tour in 1888-89, one of their stops was in Egypt, where players attempted to throw baseballs over the pyramids. Here they pose for photos on the Sphinx.

## 2 Hard Ball

Ty Cobb was a mean man back when professional baseball was a mean game. He may have been the perfect player for his time. Cobb liked to say that he would spike his grandmother if she got in his way—which was probably true. But sweet, old, grandmotherly types were not playing baseball during the early twentieth century. Baseball players were tough guys who squeezed out runs one at a time, with bunts, hit-and-run plays, sacrifices, and steals. They weren't much for home runs.

Frank "Home Run" Baker of the Philadelphia Athletics earned his nickname by leading the American League in round-trippers four years in a row. But he never hit more than 12 in any one season. Actually back then, home runs were looked down on as the products of pure muscle rather than smarts and skill.

The key was to get on base by any means possible, and then fight your way home. Ty Cobb was the best at that, maybe of all time. In 24 seasons from 1905 through 1928 (22 with the Detroit Tigers, the last two with the Philadelphia Athletics), he set over 90 major-league records. Only four other players appeared in more games than Cobb did—3,035. Only Pete Rose produced more than his 4,189 hits. Cobb is still in the top five in runs scored—doubles, triples, and stolen bases.

In the late 1950s, when a reporter asked him how he'd hit if he were playing today, Cobb said, "Oh, I'd hit .310, .315."

"But Mr. Cobb," the reporter said, "you hit over .400 three times! Why would you hit only .310 now?"

Cobb growled, "I'm 72 years old now!"

Tyrus Raymond Cobb grew up on a farm near Royston, Georgia (sportswriters nicknamed him the "Georgia Peach"). His mother was only 12 when she married his father, William, and 15 when she gave birth to Ty on December 18, 1886. William Cobb, a schoolteacher, newspaper editor, and one-time state senator and Royston mayor, had big dreams for his son. He wanted Ty to become a professional man. A lawyer or doctor would be fine, but most definitely not a professional baseball player. But it was on the ball field, not in the classroom, that Ty excelled. By 14, he was the star for the local town's team. Ty loved his father and wanted

*Opposite*: Ty Cobb rounds third base, making sure he touches the bag before he dashes for home.

## Ballparks

Ebbets Field, Brooklyn

You can play baseball almost anywhere. All you really need is a bat and a ball. You can even improvise. Sammy Sosa and Roberto Clemente used tree limbs for bats. Immigrant children in the streets of New York and Chicago in the early 1900s used rolled-up socks as balls.

Find a village green, a city park, a schoolyard, a city street, or a farmer's field, and you can figure out a way to play the game. But once baseball became an organized, professional game, teams began building baseball parks for their paying customers.

The earliest ones had wooden bleachers, mostly on the first and third base sides of the infield. Spectators would also stand down the first and third base lines or surround the outfield. Sometimes they would run onto the field, disrupting the game. Sometimes, these wooden structures caught on fire.

to make him proud, but there was tension between them. At 17, Ty left home to follow his dream.

In 1905, at 18, he was back in Georgia, in Augusta, leading the South Atlantic League in hitting, when he was called home with terrible news. His father had been killed by his mother.

According to the story Ty was told, his father suspected his much-younger wife of seeing another man and climbed a ladder to spy into her bedroom one night. Mrs. Cobb, who said she thought he was a robber trying to break in, grabbed a shotgun and shot him dead. There was a trial, and Ty's mother was acquitted of manslaughter charges. But Ty rarely saw his mother after that and did not attend her funeral.

Some baseball historians think that Cobb's fierce style of play, his quick temper, and his eagerness to take on all opponents, on and off the field, stemmed from the rage he felt over William Cobb's tragic death. Cobb himself once said, "I've never gotten over that."

Other historians have thought that Cobb was just plain crazy. But two things we know are: Ty Cobb joined the Detroit Tigers three weeks after his father died, and the game he entered was well-suited to his angry temperament.

Cobb played at a time when wooden ballparks rarely seated more than 20,000 people. Unlike today, when four umpires oversee a game, only one or two were assigned. They could barely control play on the field let alone the overflowing crowds that stood on the edges of the outfield. Fans sometimes poured onto the diamond to express their own opinions about the game.

The ball itself contributed to a game that relied on getting a run or two and holding on to the lead with good pitching. Machines simply did not exist then to wind yarn tightly enough around their rubber centers to allow them to be hit very far. Unlike today, umpires allowed pitchers to cut and discolor balls and load them up with spit and grease, a disadvantage to hitters. Batters who could bunt well, steal bases, and advance runners by hitting to all fields were in demand, but few were as good at it as Cobb.

Cobb's skill at what is now called "small ball"—to differentiate it from the current slam-bang reliance on home runs—was phenomenal. He won nine consecutive American League batting titles between 1907 and 1915, a record of 12 in all. He often led the league in stolen bases, runs scored, hits, and runs batted in. He even led the league in homers in 1909 (with nine). He led the Tigers to three World Series appearances. Yet he earned as much attention for his rough style of play as for his batting skills.

"When I began playing baseball," he once said, "baseball was about as gentlemanly as a kick in the crotch."

Cobb was a bully and an intimidator. Casey Stengel, the great Yankee manager who played in Cobb's time, said, "When he wiggled those wild eyes at a pitcher, you knew you were looking at the one bird nobody could beat. It was like he was superhuman."

Most ballplayers didn't like him, including his teammates. From the start of his career, he refused to room with anyone else and usually ate his meals alone. He rarely spoke to teammates off the field. As for opponents, he could be brutal, especially if they challenged him. He punched out several of

As major-league baseball became more popular, owners built larger ballparks made of concrete. The first one was Shibe Park, in Philadelphia. It opened in 1909. Its double-decked stands could seat 23,000 people. One year later, Charles Comiskey opened Comiskey Park in Chicago, with a capacity of 28,500. And 13 years later, Yankee Stadium opened its doors to 62,000 fans.

When major-league baseball expanded to new cities in the 1960s, another era of building ballparks took place. The most famous one was the Houston Astrodome. It was the first domed stadium. During the Houston Astros' first season, ushers dressed as astronauts to entertain the fans.

Recently, in cities like Detroit, Baltimore, and Philadelphia, owners have tried to build state-of-the-art modern ballparks that look like the old ones that were torn down in the name of progress. But you can still go to Wrigley Field in Chicago or Fenway Park in Boston and experience the real thing. Fenway was built in 1912 and seats no more than 35,000 fans. Everyone has a seat close to the field. "The Green Monster," its 37-foot-high wall, still lurks in left field.

Fenway Park, Boston

21

them, as well as fans who heckled him.

Honus Wagner, the Pittsburgh Pirates' Hall of Fame shortstop, took him on during the 1909 World Series. According to the legend, when Cobb reached first base in the first game, he yelled across the diamond to Wagner, "Watch out, Krauthead, I'm coming down. I'll cut you to pieces."

Sure enough, Cobb tried to slide spikes into Wagner, who retaliated by tagging him out—right on the mouth. (Wagner, a Hall of Famer who played 21 seasons, was a tough customer himself. Maybe it was a good thing he and Cobb were in different leagues.)

But Cobb's style was perfect for his time. Players on opposing teams, who mostly disliked him as a person, had to admire him as a competitor. His own teammates may not have liked him as a person either, but they sure liked the fact that he made them a better team. And he made the team winners, leading the Tigers to three World Series championships. He was not the strongest or fastest player in the game, but his quick mind and his ferocious intensity as a batter, fielder, and base runner would find ways to win. He worked hard at his job; he gave it his all.

Rough-and-tumble play was popular with fans in both the National and the new American League. The so-called "junior circuit" began in 1901 when Ban Johnson, an enterprising businessman, convinced a number of the National League's key players to join his new league. Cobb's Detroit team was a founding member of the American League. Baseball owners, eager to control markets and competition, worked out an agreement that led to the two major leagues that still exist today.

Up until 1961, when baseball expanded dramatically, there were only 16 teams—eight in each league. And for most of those years, 11 of those 16 teams were concentrated in only five cities! Three teams played in New York. The New York Yankees and the Brooklyn Dodgers fielded colorful and successful teams. But it was the New York Giants, led by John McGraw and Christy Mathewson, that caught the public's fancy.

McGraw was cut from the same rough cloth as Ty Cobb. A feisty, hard-nosed ballplayer with the Baltimore Orioles, he took over the Giants in 1902, quickly earning the nickname of "Little Napoleon." He was a keen baseball strategist who demanded the best from his players and got his way by making them afraid of him rather than praising and supporting them. It was ugly, but it worked, especially in those days when owners and managers had all the power. Throughout his 31-year career as the Giants's skipper, no team did it better. McGraw's boys won 10 pennants and finished third or better after 24 seasons.

*Opposite*: Always aggressive, Cobb steals second base.

A host of talented players accounted for McGraw's success. But no one was more important or more revered by him or by baseball than Christy Mathewson.

Unlike Ty Cobb, Christy Mathewson was living proof that you didn't have to be mean to make it in America's game. Baseball was America's most popular sport in the early twentieth century. Most major leaguers were uneducated farm boys from the South and Midwest or from working-class immigrant backgrounds. They played hard and lived hard and were not known for their character or their virtue.

Mathewson changed that image. He was born in 1880 to a well-to-do Scottish-American farming family in Factoryville, Pennsylvania. Christopher, or Christy, as he was called, attended private school before enrolling at Bucknell University, not far from his home. His parents hoped that he would become a minister. He stayed three years and recorded an excellent academic record. But he did even better on the football field and on the baseball diamond. In 1901 he signed on with the New York Giants. Blond-haired, blue-eyed, and married to a Sunday-school teacher, he was hailed by the press as "the Christian Gentleman," and popularly known by the nickname "Matty."

In an era of dominant pitchers that included Walter "Big Train" Johnson and Grover Cleveland Alexander, none was more prominent than Matty for his sportsmanship and courage as well as his pitching prowess—373 wins, the third highest total in major-league history; an earned run average (ERA) of 2.13, the fifth best ever; and three straight shutout victories in the 1905 World Series. He was voted into the Hall of Fame's first class of inductees in 1936, along

*Above*: Legendary Pittsburgh shortstop Honus Wagner makes sure his bat is in good shape.

with Cobb, Babe Ruth, Johnson, and Wagner. Matty's shining virtues became more important after the so-called "Black Sox" scandal threatened to damage the popularity of the game.

This incident concerned gamblers trying to "fix" the outcome of the 1919 World Series. The journalists who covered the story reserved their harshest criticism for the players involved. Not for the gamblers who set up the scheme. Not for the team owners who made conditions so horrible for the players that they were tempted by the gamblers' money. Because gamblers, after all, were criminals and were expected to act

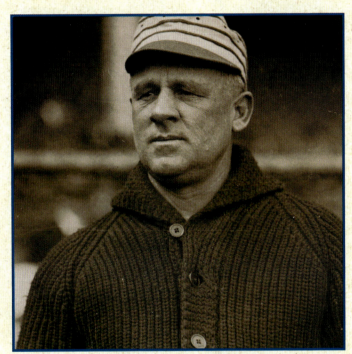

that way. And the team owners, after all, were businessmen who were expected to maximize the profit they made from the team. But the players were held to a higher standard, because they were supposed to represent not only the best attributes of professional athletes, but of all Americans. They were heroes in the public's eye, and they betrayed that trust. And it is tragic when national heroes fall from grace.

The 1919 World Series pitted the Cincinnati Reds against the Chicago White Sox, whose most famous player was "Shoeless Joe" Jackson, a South Carolina country boy who got his nickname because he once took off his too-tight shoes and played a minor-league game in his stockinged feet.

Shoeless Joe couldn't read or write, but he sure could hit, especially with the bat he nicknamed "Black Betsy." With Joe in the lineup, the World Series was supposed to be no contest. But there was discontent on the White Sox. Players did not like one another and most of them hated Charles Comiskey, the penny-pinching owner who underpaid them. He even refused to pay to have their uniforms cleaned. That's when the players began calling themselves the Black Sox.

Chick Gandil, the White Sox first baseman, came up with the idea to intentionally let Cincinnati, the underdog, win the World Series. Seven teammates, including Joe and the club's two best pitchers, Eddie

*Above*: John McGraw, manager of the New York Giants, put together winning rosters for 27 years.

Cicotte and "Lefty" Claude Williams, agreed to participate. Gamblers promised the ball players $100,000 for making sure Chicago lost. The gamblers would bet against Chicago and make a fortune. The gamblers who put up the cash included Joseph "Sport" Sullivan; Abe Attell, a former featherweight boxing champion; and perhaps Arnold Rothstein, one of New York's most prominent gangsters. (In the end they cheated the players, too, giving them only $40,000.)

In those days, the World Series was a best-of-nine contest instead of the current seven games. The winning team needed to win five of the nine games.

Chicago lost the first two games. They won the third, behind the masterful pitching of Dickie Kerr, a rookie who was not in on the fix. Then they dropped the next two games. Newspaper reporters wondered out loud about the poor play of some of Chicago's stars. Joe Jackson's name was never mentioned. In fact, he batted .375 for the entire series, hit a home run, and never made an error in the outfield.

Cincinnati needed only one more victory to clinch the series. But when the gamblers failed to come up with the rest of the money

> "You gotta be careful with your body. Your body is like a bar of soap. The more you use it, the more it wears down."
> —Richie Allen, Phillies slugger

they owed the ballplayers, the conspiracy seemed to collapse. Chicago won the next two games. With Lefty Williams scheduled to pitch the next game, the White Sox looked to tie the series at four games each. It never happened. Intimidated by a Chicago hoodlum who threatened to harm the pitcher and his family, Williams gave up three runs on four consecutive hits in the first inning. The White Sox eventually lost the game 10-5 and the series, five games to three.

Christy Mathewson, by this time retired, reported on the series for the *New York Evening World*. On his scorecards, he carefully noted instances where Chicago's play seemed suspect, although he wrote nothing about his suspicions in his columns.

Other reporters were less cautious. Ring Lardner, one of this country's most famous sportswriters, then writing for the *Chicago Tribune*, even blasted the Sox in song. His spoof of a popular ditty about bubbles went like this: "I'm forever blowing ball games, pretty ball games in the air; I come from Chi, I hardly try, Just go to bat to fade and die; fortune's coming my way,

*Opposite: Christy Mathewson of the Giants was the best pitcher of his era.*

that's why I don't care. I'm forever blowing ball games, and the gamblers treat us fair."

In the days before radio and television, professional baseball had become one of the most popular forms of entertainment in the country, attracting a peak of five million fans through the turnstiles in 1917. During the World Series, thousands of people gathered at hotels and public spaces in cities throughout the country to follow the games as they were reported by telegraph. But attendance had dropped to three million by 1919 as the country, still reeling from World War I, found less time for mere amusement. Now, rumors of scandal threatened to destroy the integrity of the game. The Black Sox scandal remained in the news for more than a year, damaging the game's standing and its business potential.

In September 1920, a grand jury was convened in Chicago to look into claims that Chicago's other team, the Cubs, had thrown games with the Philadelphia Athletics. The investigation spread to include the 1919 World Series. Three Chicago ballplayers testified before the grand jury and admitted their guilt.

One player was Shoeless Joe, who reported that he had received $5,000 out of a promised $20,000 for being in on the fix. It has become legend that a young boy rushed

over to his fallen idol when he stepped out of the courthouse and said, "Say it ain't so, Joe."

"Yes, kid, I'm afraid it is," Joe replied.

Soon after, the phrase "Say it ain't so, Joe," became a popular American saying.

Grand juries investigate suspected crimes, but they do not decide whether or not a person is guilty. By the time the case came to trial in 1921, the confessions of the three ballplayers had mysteriously disappeared. (Had someone destroyed them for the good of the game?) On August 2, 1921, all the ballplayers and the gamblers were found to be not guilty.

But that wasn't good enough for Kenesaw Mountain Landis, professional baseball's first commissioner. The next day,

*Above:* "Shoeless" Joe Jackson took money to throw the 1919 World Series, but his statistics suggest that he played to win.

he banned the players for life. Judge Landis had been recently appointed to his new job by baseball owners who were eager to show that baseball still deserved its reputation as America's national game.

Landis certainly felt it did. "Baseball," he said, "is something more than a game to an American boy. It is his training field for life work. Destroy his faith in its squareness and honesty and you have destroyed something more; you have planted suspicion in his heart."

Landis believed that by banning corrupt ballplayers, baseball would remain pure. And it would encourage fans to return to the ballparks. Not everyone agreed that the punishment fit the supposed crime. Even Christy Mathewson thought the lifetime ban too harsh.

So did Joe Jackson, who continued to play baseball under assumed names for the next decade. Although Joe did admit that he took money from gamblers, no one ever could point to a single play during the World Series where he had let his teammates down. His glorious statistics during the series matched his lifetime major-league batting average of .356. By the numbers alone, this shy, soft-spoken, considerate

man belongs next to Christy Mathewson and Ty Cobb in baseball's Hall of Fame.

But the people who run baseball have always believed that the integrity of the game must never be in question. Fans have to be able to believe that what they are watching is honest, that players are trying their best. This is why baseball never forgave Joe Jackson for becoming involved in the Black Sox scandal.

Ty Cobb remained one of baseball's reigning superstars before, during, and after the Black Sox scandal. He played hurt, played to win, did whatever it took on the field, and expected nothing less from his teammates. If Shoeless Joe could no longer be seen as a hero to young baseball fans, Cobb, despite his aggressive, nasty personality could. No one could ever imagine Cobb being tempted—by *anything*—to intentionally lose a game.

> "Slow thinkers are part of the game, too. Some of these slow thinkers can hit a ball a long way."
> —Alvin Dark, Giant shortstop

# ③ The Gift of the Bambino

It was a crucial time for baseball in America. Fans, players, owners, and the press worried about the integrity and the future of the nation's pastime. Fortunately at that moment, another player took center stage, the likes of whom had never been seen before. He was a larger-than-life figure who loved the game and played it like a man among boys. His amazing feats on the field became legendary, and he became the icon of baseball for the entire world. He would acquire several nicknames during his baseball career, but most people simply knew him as the "Babe."

Babe Ruth made America forget about the Black Sox and the small-ball tough guys who had dominated baseball before him, just when the country was ready to cut loose and have some fun.

"The Sultan of Swat," as Ruth was dubbed, was more than just a ballplayer. Loud and warmhearted, his style and personality came to symbolize America in his time, the Roaring Twenties. The country, having recovered from World War I, was filled with ordinary people who now had some leisure time and the money to purchase a new Ford, see a movie, buy something at a department store, and go to a baseball game on a sunny summer afternoon. Spend, consume, enjoy.

That's just how the Babe lived his life. He loved to eat, drink, and party. But there was more to his life. He also reminded people of an earlier time in our country's history when hard work and individualism counted the most. Not bad for a boy who was raised in an orphanage because his parents didn't want him. It wasn't until he was a celebrity and applied for a passport that he found out his date of birth!

George Herman Ruth was born in Baltimore, Maryland, on February 6, 1895, at the home of his maternal grandfather. He was one of eight children born to George Sr. and Kate Ruth. Only two of them lived to become adults.

The Ruths were a tired, angry couple. Sometimes they took out their frustrations by beating their young son. They had no time for little George, who grew up wild on the streets. He stole from stores, skipped school, and chewed tobacco. He drank whiskey and "hated the coppers." He threw apples and eggs at truck drivers.

*Opposite*: Ruth enjoyed baseball as much as anyone who played the game. He just did it a bit better than everyone else.

"I honestly don't remember being aware of the difference between right and wrong," Ruth once said. "I was a bum when I was a kid. I hardly knew my parents. I had a rotten start, and it took me a long time to get my bearings."

When he was seven years old, his parents committed him to the Catholic St. Mary's Industrial School for Boys as an "incorrigible"—which meant they were just giving up on him. He spent most of the next eight years at St. Mary's. It turned out to be his salvation because the school never gave up on him.

St. Mary's was run by the Xavierian Brothers. It was a reform school and orphanage for 800 boys between the ages of five and twenty-one. Everyone was kept busy from sunup to sundown. There was attending chapel, doing chores, and getting basic schooling. The boys even spent time learning how to be everything from a shirtmaker to a plumber. Most importantly for George, there was always baseball and other sports to fill out the day.

Ruth arrived as a gawky, unattractive boy. In a country where segregation was still legal and where African Americans were denied full equality, his schoolmates tagged him with the racist nickname "Niggerlips." By the time he left, no one dared call him that to his face. In

ten years he grew to be 6'2" tall, with 180 pounds of rippling muscle, much of it in his powerful chest and shoulders.

Ruth barely learned to read or write at St. Mary's. But he did learn how to make shirts and how to play baseball. Brother Matthias, a former athlete and one of the teachers who took a particular interest in the boy, made sure of that. They would spend hours together, hitting and catching and talking about the game.

Much like a young A. G. Spalding, Ruth gained acceptance among his peers by his play on the field. He played catcher and pitched. And could he hit! In his last year at St. Mary's, Ruth did not lose a single game on the mound and hit at least one home run in every game he played. By then, he also was playing for local semipro and amateur teams.

In 1914 Jack Dunn signed him to a contract with the Baltimore Orioles—a once powerful National League franchise which had become a minor-league club—for $100 a month, a standard beginner's wage at that time. Because Dunn saw future greatness in the rookie and spent a lot of time helping him improve, Ruth became known as Dunn's "baby." The nickname stuck and was shortened to "Babe."

But Dunn became desperate for cash to save his team from bankruptcy. Reluctantly he sold Ruth to the Boston Red Sox that same year. Babe stayed in Boston for six seasons and became the left-handed pitching ace of a fine staff. In his first four full years there he won 78 games and lost 34, compiling an ERA of 2.05. The Red Sox won the World Series in three of those years. The young Ruth batted .315 in 1915 and hit four of his team's 14 home runs. Switched to the outfield in 1919 to take advantage of his batting skills, Ruth belted 29 round-trippers.

At the close of that season, Harry Frazee, the Red Sox's owner, eager for money to invest in Broadway musicals, sold the budding star to the New York Yankees for $125,000. It was the most money ever paid for a player, and a bargain. The rest, as they say, is history. It was the start of a great Yankees team and soon the greatest dynasty in sports. It was also the end of the Boston Red Sox's domination. The Red Sox did not win another World Series after selling Ruth until 2004. (Fittingly, they had to overcome a three-games-to-none advantage by the Yankees to win the American League pennant and the right to compete in the World Series, which they swept from the St. Louis Cardinals.)

Fans everywhere enjoyed the gift of the Bambino, which was a new kind of baseball. No more squeezing out one run at a time. Babe Ruth, the King of Clout, made baseball a power game where a last-inning home run could turn everything upside down.

The Babe was the top player in America's top sport—a human superpower! With one mighty swing, the Babe could win a game. He was a commanding force, just like his country. He could also eat more, drink more, and play harder than anyone else in sports. Yet as powerful as he was, he was friendly

## Baseball Movies

A scene from *Field of Dreams*

Here are some of my favorite baseball movies. Go to your local library or video store and see for yourself!

1. Bull Durham (1988)

2. It Happens Every Spring (1949)

3. The Natural (1984)

4. Field of Dreams (1989)

5. Bingo Long's Traveling All-Stars and Motor Kings (1976)

6. The Bad News Bears (1976)

7. Eight Men Out (1988)

8. A League of Their Own (1992)

9. Major League (1989)

superb pitchers and a batting order of great hitters known as "Murderers' Row." Waite Hoyt, Herb Pennock, and Urban Shocker were the stars of the mound and such sluggers as Tony Lazzeri and Bob Meusel were capable of "five o'clock lightning," the sportswriters' nickname for the Yankees' late-inning rallies, game-winning homers in those afternoon-only contests.

Overshadowed by Ruth but almost as important to the team was Lou Gehrig, the first baseman known as the "Iron Horse," who was the handsome, quiet, humble son of German immigrants. Raised in New York, Gehrig had played football at Columbia University. Gehrig hit .373 with 47 homers in 1927, the year that Ruth hit 60, the record that stood for 34 years. Gehrig's own famous record of 2,130 consecutive games ended when he took himself out of the line-up in 1939 because he felt weak; he was soon diagnosed with amyotrophic lateral sclerosis, a degenerative disease that would take his life two years later. It is now commonly known as Lou Gehrig's disease.

On July 4, 1939, the Yankees celebrated his forced retirement with Lou Gehrig Day. There, before a packed house, Lou gave an emotional farewell speech that baseball fans still recall. He started by saying that "today I can say that I consider myself the luckiest man on the face of the earth."

and kind. And he cared about little kids and elderly people, going out of his way to stop by and say hello to the very young and very old at orphanages and retirement homes. He was fun to watch, and people flocked to the ballpark.

The Babe was also a perfect fit for the Yankees at that time. Babe led the team to six pennants and three World Series victories in the 1920s, with some help from

*Above*: Herb Pennock was one of the star pitchers for the Yankees teams of the 1920s. *Opposite*: Lou Gehrig, called the "Iron Horse" because he rarely missed a game, was as good a hitter as the Babe.

Gehrig was the top Yankees hitter after Ruth retired and the leader of another Yankee dynasty. But he performed in the Babe's huge shadow as did all the other sluggers of Ruth's time.

At the same time that Ruth was performing his legendary feats for the Yankees, another amazing ballplayer was tearing up the National League.

Rogers Hornsby was considered the greatest right-handed hitter of his time and perhaps the greatest in history (the Babe was left-handed). He retired in 1937 after 23 seasons, mostly with the St. Louis Cardinals, with a .358 average and 301 home runs. His 1924 batting average, .424, is the modern record. A hard-bitten loud-mouth from Texas, Hornsby played various infield positions and led the Cards to the 1926 World Series victory over Ruth and the Yankees. Hornsby said that he never went to the movies when

he was a player because he wanted to keep his batting eye sharp. And he certainly did.

Jimmie Foxx, nicknamed "Beast" and "Double XX," was another right-handed Hall of Fame slugger who went after the Babe's mantle. In 20 seasons, starting in 1925 with the Philadelphia Athletics, he batted .325 and hit 534 homers. He also played for the Red Sox, the Cubs, and the Phillies, mostly at first base.

Hornsby and Foxx were idolized by young and old fans alike. They were also instrumental in helping baseball recover from the black mark of the 1919 World Series. They were the new heroes of the game, but despite their skills and achieve-ments, they could never topple Ruth from the pedestal the public had placed him on. As long as Ruth played, he remained king.

By the time the Babe retired from baseball after 22 seasons, he had set 56 major-league

*Above*: Babe Ruth became the face of baseball that was known all around the world.

> "I think about the cosmic snowball theory. A few million years from now the Sun will burn out and lose its gravitational pull. The Earth will turn into a giant snowball and be hurled through space. When that happens it won't matter if I got this guy out."
> —Bill "Spaceman" Lee, Red Sox pitcher

records, including most home runs in a season (60), most home runs in a career (714), most seasons with 40 home runs or more (11), most walks in a single season (170 in 1923), most strikeouts in a career (1,330), highest career slugging average (.690), and most runs batted in (2,213).

After 1922 his team played its home games in the newly constructed Yankee Stadium, which became known as "the house that Ruth built." It was the biggest and best ballpark in the major leagues, with a seating capacity of 58,000. With a wonderful sense of drama, the Bambino hit a home run his second time up on opening day.

"I swing as hard as I can, and I try to swing right through the ball," said the Babe. "I swing big, with everything I've got. I hit big or I miss big. I like to live as big as I can."

That was the Babe, the "Hero of Too Much in an Age of Too Much." In the Roaring Twenties, with its booming economy, its vast natural resources, and a large and growing immigrant labor pool, America was boisterous and confident.

So was the Babe. People loved to follow his exploits. He was a loud, lovable man who didn't have a mean bone in his body. Babe could be crude, even rude. He had a hard time remembering anyone's name, so he often called his teammates "kid." But he also liked to visit sick children in hospitals, and he was generous with his time and money.

Because readers loved him and he was such a good story, sportswriters never reported on his wild carousing. When he had hangovers they were reported as bellyaches from too many hotdogs.

In some ways, Babe was the model for great modern sports superstars like Tiger Woods and Michael Jordan. He was the first sports celebrity to have his own agent, and he made more money outside of baseball than from his salary from playing. Coming along when talking movies first made their appearance, Babe starred in *The Babe Comes Home,* a feature film made in 1927. Ghostwritten sports columns and children's

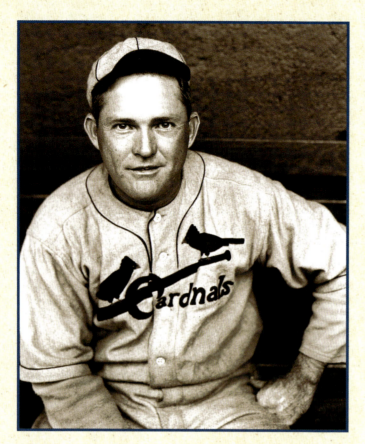

future. But mostly they struggled simply to put food on the table and keep a roof over their heads. African Americans still lived under harsh discrimination that denied them any chance of their American dreams.

Babe offered them all hope. If he could make it, they could. At least that's what he

books, appearances on the vaudeville circuit and on the radio, and endorsements from everything from cigarettes to automobiles made him close to $2 million during the course of his career, fabulous money in those days. He spent it, too.

Babe's appeal was universal. People with the money to enjoy what an abundant America had to offer found him attractive. But so did those Americans who were not prosperous. The new waves of Italian and Jewish immigrants living in crowded city slums may well have dreamed of a glowing

*Above*: Rogers Hornsby, perhaps the greatest right-handed hitter in baseball history. But he was overshadowed by the Babe.
*Above, right*: Babe Ruth, on tour with all-stars in Japan, puts on a show for the crowd.

told them in his autobiography: "The greatest thing about this country is the wonderful fact that it doesn't matter what side of the tracks you were born on or whether you're homeless or friendless. The chance is still there. I know."

People wanted to believe that. Hank Greenberg, the great Detroit Tigers slugger of the 1930s, grew up in New York. He remembered that Ruth was every boy's hero in his Jewish neighborhood. When Hank became an established star, Jewish fans across the country called Greenberg "the Jewish Babe Ruth." Even many African Americans wondered out loud whether the racist nickname of the Babe's youth might just be proof that he was black like them!

As the Roaring Twenties collapsed into the Great Depression of the 1930s, with people out of work lining up for free bread, Ruth's excesses were not so loveable any more, and his $80,000 salary—he was the highest-paid player in the game—suddenly seemed like too much.

The Yankees let him go after the 1934 season. In 1935, at 40 years old, he played a disappointing season with the Boston Braves. He died in 1948, at 53, of throat cancer.

But the memory of Babe Ruth lives on. With his bat and his grin he revived baseball in its darkest hour and played the game with the joy of the kids who came to watch him.

*Above*: Jimmie Foxx played mostly at first base. Here he shows his fielding prowess with a catcher's mitt.

# 4 The First

It was a day that caused the nation to hold its breath. On April 15, 1947, a handsome, smart, 28-year-old named Jack Roosevelt Robinson walked out to first base at Ebbets Field in New York. He was wearing the uniform of the Brooklyn Dodgers, but on his shoulders he carried the goal of equal opportunity for all Americans. Jack Roosevelt Robinson was African American, the first to play in the modern major leagues.

Not everyone wanted him to succeed. America was still segregated by law then. Baseball was ahead of most of the rest of the country in admitting its first African-American player. As one famous civil rights leader, the Reverend Jesse Jackson, would later say, "The fate of a race rode on his swing."

Maybe even the fate of the *country* rode on his swing. How could we think of ourselves as a land of freedom and fair play if our national pastime wasn't open to all? Can you imagine the burden of playing with that on your mind? It's hard enough just to make contact with a major-league pitch without worrying about how important it is that you get a hit.

These days, when so many of our greatest athletes in all sports are African Americans, it's hard to imagine the importance of that singular moment in 1947.

"Jackie gave us our dreams," said Hank Aaron, the black Hall of Famer who, 27 years after Jackie's debut, would rewrite one of baseball's most cherished statistics by breaking Babe Ruth's all-time career record for home runs.

We think of Jackie Robinson as an historical figure, but he would never have been able to blaze a trail in human rights if he hadn't also been able to blaze a trail around the base paths. Jackie was fast enough to take long leads and make risky steals. He stole home *19 times* in his 10-year career. He could hit with home-run power and he was a terrific infielder. He was a fierce competitor who never gave up until the last out. As a member of the Yankees who had played against Robinson, Hall of Famer Yogi Berra said it best: "He could beat you a lot of ways."

Jackie played hard as a kid. While teachers and friends, who knew him growing up in Pasadena, California, remembered him as friendly and charming, he could also be a hard-nosed competitor on the ballfield. "His whole thing was just win, win, win, and beat everybody," said a friend from those days.

*Opposite:* In 1946 Jackie Robinson reports to the Dodgers farm team in Montreal.

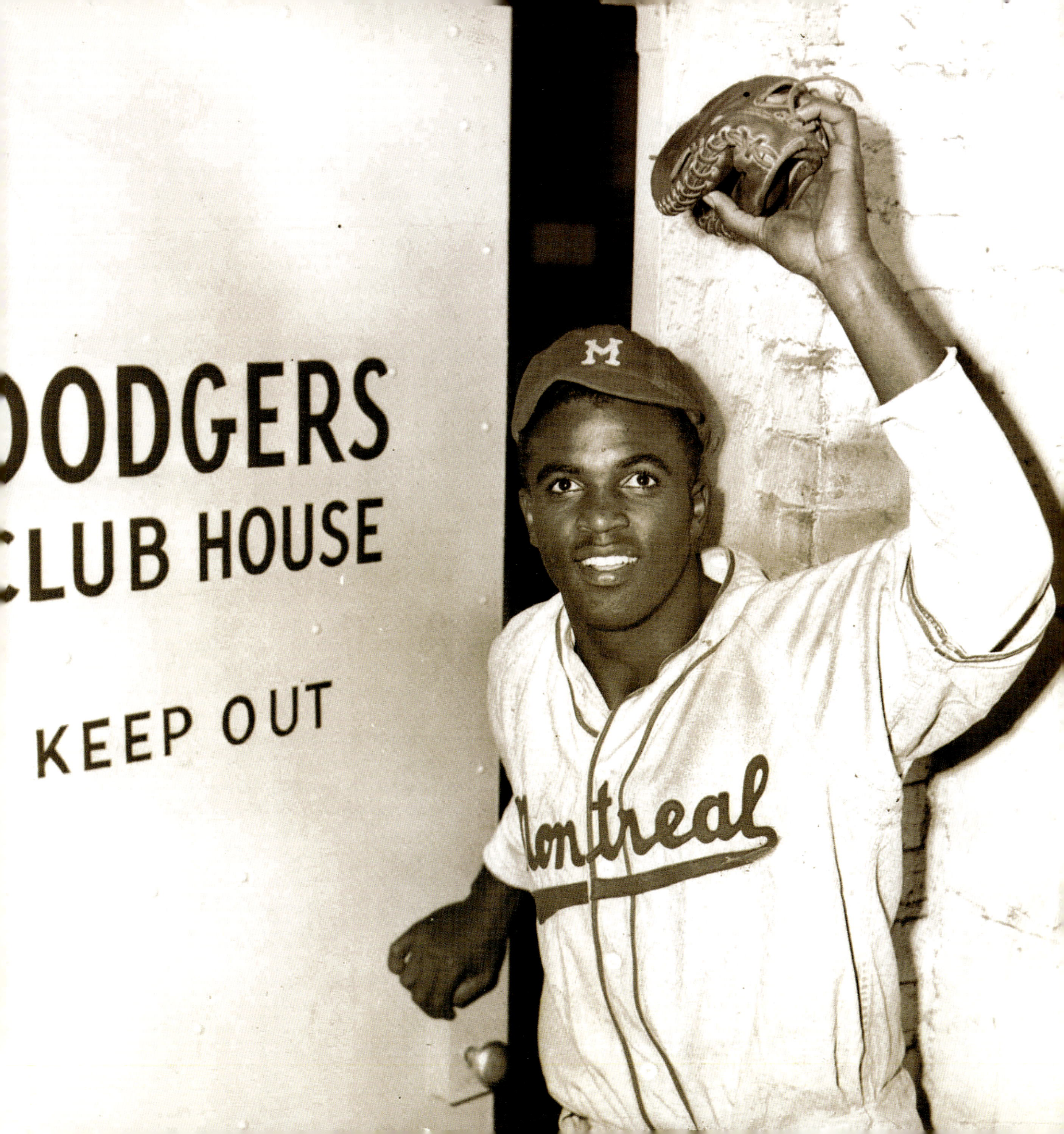
ODGERS
CLUB HOUSE
KEEP OUT
M
Montreal

## The Negro Leagues

In 1933 the National Negro League (NNL) was formed. It was not the first all-black league, but it was the most successful. Its best teams were the Kansas City Monarchs, and 2 clubs located in Pittsburgh, the Crawfords and the Homestead Grays. It also had clubs in other cities with large black, urban populations such as Chicago, New York, Philadelphia, Newark, and Baltimore.

These teams were the pride of their communities. Their players were local heroes who gave youngsters and parents hope at a time when African Americans were denied the chance to fulfill their American dreams because of the color of their skin. NNL teams played a full schedule of games and had their own World Series. Their midseason all-star game, usually played at Comiskey Park, Chicago, was the highlight of the season. More than

Satchel Paige

There were people who knew Jackie was special, long before he put on a major-league uniform. The grandson of a slave and the son of a cleaning woman, Jackie became one of the finest all-around athletes at the University of California at Los Angeles. He starred in football, basketball, and golf as well as baseball, and he competed successfully in tennis and swimming. Jackie went on to become an officer in the segregated United States Army during World War II. After his major-league career, Jackie was an important business executive, civil rights activist, and political figure in New York.

But first, he was The First.

Even now, when people want to describe someone as a brave pioneer, they call that person the "Jackie Robinson of . . ." Think of striding into dangerous territory where no one like you has ever gone before; where the people, rooting for you to fall on your face, will try to knock you over; and the people rooting for you to succeed will make you nervous. Imagine how strong you would have to be, mentally as well as physically, to make it under such circumstances.

That's why Jackie Robinson was picked to be The First. He wasn't the best black ballplayer of his time. But he might have been the ballplayer with the strongest will to succeed—black or white.

The white baseball executive who picked him to be The First deserves credit for bravery, too. His name was Branch Rickey, and he was the general manager of the Brooklyn Dodgers. He was a moral man who believed all Americans should have equal opportunities. He was also a practical man who knew there were hundreds of gifted black professional ballplayers on Negro League teams in America, and there were thousands, maybe millions, of black fans who would pay to see them play on major-league teams.

In 1945, right after the end of World War II, baseball commissioner Happy Chandler declared that if black men "could fight and die" for America, they should be able to play major-league baseball, too. But Chandler could not convince the club owners. The next year, the club owners voted 15-1 to keep their game all-white.

That one vote, of course, was Branch Rickey's. He tried to persuade the other owners that not only was it right for black men to play major-league baseball, it was good business. But segregation had been in place for a long time. They refused to listen, so Rickey made a plan.

Rickey understood that he might have only one chance to break the color barrier, so he needed to find exactly the right person. His scouts kept coming up with the name Jack Roosevelt Robinson.

Jackie's seasons as a UCLA athlete had given him experience playing with and against white men. And Jackie proved he could play high-level pro-ball. After the army, he played for a season with the Kansas City Monarchs, the best team in the Negro Leagues. Since blacks were not allowed to play in the major leagues, the competition in the Negro Leagues was intense. White major leaguers admitted that there were Negro leaguers better than many of them. Jackie led his team with a .345 batting average.

The only question was about Jackie's temper. He was a fierce competitor who never backed down. He was a fighter. Could he control his anger at the racial hatred that would surely come his way?

Rickey has become a legend. Because Rickey was

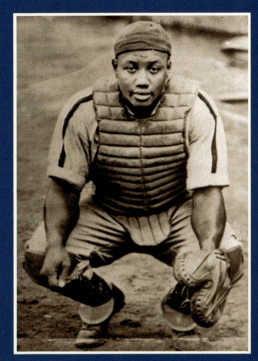

Josh Gibson

50,000 fans, dressed in their best clothes, packed the ballpark to celebrate the skill and daring of the league's best players.

Players like Josh Gibson, Cool Papa Bell, Oscar Charleston, Buck Leonard, Smokey Joe Williams, and the great Satchel Paige were surely as talented as the best that the major leagues had to offer. They proved it in the off-season, when teams of black and white all-stars played one another in exhibition games all over the country.

No player was more famous than Satchel. Including Negro League teams, exhibition games, and a brief stint in the major leagues, it's estimated that between 1926 and 1950, Paige pitched in some 2,500 games! His longest stints in the NNL were with Pittsburgh and Kansas City.

The NNL collapsed in the 1940s, when black ballplayers began to play in the major leagues.

keeping his plan a secret, even from Robinson, the ballplayer thought he was being interviewed for a new Negro League team sponsored by the Brooklyn Dodgers. So when Rickey asked Jackie if he thought he could play in the major leagues, Robinson, surprised, blurted, "Yes."

Rickey barked: "I know you're a good ballplayer. What I don't know is if you have the guts."

For the next three hours, Rickey lectured and harangued. He talked about social justice and beanballs—opposing pitchers would throw at Jackie's head and base runners would try to spike him. This was bigger than baseball. There would be constant attacks: verbal, psychological, and physical. Jackie would have to turn the other cheek, control his well-known temper, and not fight back.

"Mr. Rickey," Jackie asked, "are you looking for a Negro who is afraid to fight back?"

"Robinson," said Rickey, "I am looking for a ballplayer with guts enough not to fight back."

For two long, tough years, Robinson turned the other cheek. He spent the 1946 season with the Dodgers' best minor-league team, the Montreal Royals. Just as Rickey predicted, Jackie faced prejudice and racial slurs from opposing players and fans. But Montreal's fans were delighted with him and his wife, Rachel, who worked as a psychiatric nurse. Jackie batted .349 and led the Royals to the International League championship. He thrilled spectators with his dazzling speed and daring base running, and with his coolness under pressure.

In a game in Syracuse, opposing players threw a black cat on the field and yelled, "Here's your cousin."

At his next at-bat, Robinson doubled and scored. He then sauntered past the Syracuse dugout and said, "I guess my cousin's happy now."

Jackie was ready for the big leagues.

But not everyone in the big leagues was ready for him. The St. Louis Cardinals warned that they might refuse to play if Jackie took the field. There was hate mail and threats to kidnap Robinson's son. A Dodgers teammate, pitcher Hugh Casey, was one of several Southerners who said they would quit if they had to play with a black man. They backed off, grumbling, when Rickey simply said he would accept their resignations.

Jackie Robinson had a difficult time.

> "Always follow your dream, don't let anyone tell you that you can't be something."
> —Alex Rodriguez, Yankee third baseman

Fans, who wanted him to fail, tried to intimidate him. They cursed him and sent him death threats. Other ballplayers, including some of his own teammates, said they would strike if he played. There was a barrage of racial slurs from opposing dugouts. Some opposing pitchers threw at his head. Base runners tried to spike him.

That first big-league game was something of a disappointment—in four at-bats, Jackie grounded out twice, once into a double-play, flied out to left field, and got on base when his bunt was booted for an error. But just showing up was a victory. And Jackie was tough. In the history of American sports, no athlete has ever performed so well under such great pressure. The rest of that first season was a sensational success. Robinson was voted Rookie of the Year for both leagues and led the Dodgers into the World Series.

Robinson's grace, his talent, his refusal to get rattled, his willingness to suffer silently, helped win over his teammates. They rallied round him. The Kentucky-born shortstop, Pee Wee Reese, was particularly important. During some of the worst moments, Reese would put his white hand on Robinson's shoulder in a very public display of friendship. Late in the season, when one of the Cardinals went out of his way to spike Jackie, it was Hugh Casey who led the Dodgers, roaring out of their dugout to defend their teammate.

"I had started the season as a lonely man," Jackie wrote years later in an autobiography, "often feeling like a black Don Quixote tilting at white windmills. I ended it feeling like a member of a solid team."

His rookie season was a success in every way. He was a box-office sensation, paying back his $5,000 salary at least 100 times over by packing the Dodgers' Ebbets Field. He was a popular sensation; one poll had him as the second best-liked man in America, after the white singer Bing Crosby. He was a moral sensation, making decent white folks feel good about themselves and giving black folks a new sense of pride and inspiration.

That next spring, in Mobile, Alabama, a high school boy named Henry cut classes to

*Above*: Brooklyn Dodgers' owner, Branch Rickey, signs Jackie Robinson to his first major-league contract.

death threats. The memory of Jackie's courage, he said, gave him the strength to ignore them and slug on. He broke the old record of 714 on April 8, 1974, and eventually set the new record of 755.

A year later, another Robinson achieved another first in baseball. In 1975, Frank Robinson, related to Jackie only in fighting spirit, became the first African-American manager, taking charge of the Cleveland Indians. Frank Robinson had great credentials. He'd been voted Rookie of the Year in 1956 and was the only man ever named Most Valuable Player in both leagues (with the Reds in 1961 and the Orioles in 1966). He was a slugger, an aggressive outfielder, and a hard-charging base runner who would later be voted into the Hall of Fame. But there were people then who believed that white ballplayers wouldn't take orders from a black manager. They were wrong, of course. As with Jackie Robinson, it wasn't about color but about strength of will.

hear Jackie talk to local kids in a downtown drugstore. The Dodgers were in town for an exhibition game, and Jackie always made time to speak with black kids.

"I can't remember exactly what he said, but I do know my mouth was wide open," said Hank Aaron, years later. "I was in the back, but I felt like I was hugging him, you know? Holding his hand. I saw a concerned citizen. He was saying something like, 'Hey, just give yourself a chance. If I can make it, all of you can make it. It may not be in sports, but it can be in something.'"

In the early 1970s, during Hank Aaron's campaign to break Babe Ruth's career record of 714 home runs, he began to get vicious hate mail filled with racial slurs and

The spirit of Jackie sustained the black players who followed him. Later in 1947, the Cleveland Indians signed a superb outfielder and hitter, Larry Doby, who led the team to two American League pennants and the 1948 World Series championship. After his major-league career was over, Doby, and another African American, the Dodger pitcher Don Newcombe, became the first former major-league stars to play for a

*Above*: Happy Chandler was the first baseball commissioner to try to integrate the game.

professional Japanese team, the Chunichi Dragons in 1962.

When other African-American stars such as Roy Campanella, Monte Irvin, Joe Black, and Junior Gilliam joined Jackie as major league players, more racial attitudes and barriers were broken. With that battle having essentially been won, Jackie returned to his natural personality, the fighter with a quick temper.

By 1949, Jackie was no longer turning the other cheek. His natural inclination as a person, a ballplayer, and an activist for human rights was to fight back, sometimes to start the action. From acting humble and quiet (a constant struggle for him), Jackie quickly earned a new reputation among umpires and opposing ballplayers as a hothead and a troublemaker. He played with reckless abandon, and he took no guff. The real Jackie was even better than the deceptively meek Jackie. In his third year he was selected as the National League's most valuable player. He collected 124 runs batted in, while leading the league with 37 stolen bases and a .342 batting average.

Jackie retired from major-league baseball in 1956. In 1962 he became the first African-American ballplayer ever to be elected to baseball's Hall of Fame. His legacy was apparent: In the ten years after he became major-league baseball's Most Valuable Player, black men won the award eight times. And in the ten-year span from 1960-

1970, there were seven black National League rookies of the year. Branch Rickey had been right about the enormous pool of talented black athletes.

Off the field, Jackie was an early supporter of Dr. Martin Luther King Jr. and a member of the National Association for the Advancement of Colored People (NAACP). As a business executive for one of the first popular fast-food chains, Chock Full O' Nuts (also the brand of a popular coffee), he encouraged the hiring of black workers and executives.

He also kept his eye on the new

*Above*: Roy Campanella, Jackie's teammate, was one of the great African-American players to benefit from Robinson's courage.

Why? Ask Frank Robinson, the first black manager. Jackie made it possible for him and other minority managers, coaches, and executives to find their rightful places in the national pastime. Ask Curt Flood, the brave African-American outfielder who challenged the way baseball wrote its contracts; it was the fighting spirit of Jackie that improved conditions for all players.

generation of black athletes. Ernie Banks, the Chicago Cubs' Hall of Fame shortstop, remembers Jackie taking him aside during his rookie year and advising him to get rid of the flashy gold cap on his front tooth. Jackie told him that he was a role model now, and he should look like one.

Jackie died in 1972 from the complications of diabetes, a disease made more severe by stress, which he certainly had. He was only 53. His wife, who keeps his legacy alive in a foundation that supports education for black youth and fights discrimination, wonders if the pressures of being The First took their toll.

His number—42—has been officially retired by every major-league baseball team, the first and only tribute of its kind.

And ask any baseball fan how much better the game—and America—became once Jackie moved us all closer to a level playing field.

*Above*: Jackie Robinson steals home during a game. *Above, right*: Jackie worked with Martin Luther King Jr., on social issues in the 1960s. *Opposite*: A happy Dodgers' clubhouse in 1952 featured (*from left to right*) shortstop Pee Wee Reese, Jackie Robinson, and pitcher Preacher Roe. Roe had just beaten the Yankees in game three of the '52 World Series.

# 5 The Mick

The search for the next Babe Ruth, another slugging outfielder who could win games with his bat and fans with his personality, has been going on ever since the original Babe ended his legendary career. Nobody has ever replaced the Bambino. But a few have come close, and Mickey Mantle probably closest of all.

Mantle was the prototypical all-American baseball hero. First of all he looked the part. He was a towheaded, gray-eyed farm boy from Oklahoma. He had good looks, an easy smile, and an impressive build—5'11" and 195 pounds of solid muscle.

The ultimate compliment often paid to a baseball player is to say that he is a "five-tool player." This means he has above-average speed; he is an excellent fielder; he has a strong throwing arm; he can hit for average; and he can hit for power. Mantle had all five tools, and then some. He had a sprinter's speed; he was an excellent bunter as well as a home-run threat; and he was a switch-hitter with devastating power from both sides of the plate.

He came to the Yankees with great expectations—from the management and from the fans. Following Babe Ruth would have been difficult enough. Mantle followed not only Ruth but a second all-star outfielder for the Yankees, Joe DiMaggio, who was so good he had almost made New York forget about the Bambino.

DiMaggio had joined the Yankees in 1936, just one year after the Babe retired, and was an immediate star, hitting .323 (his lifetime average over 13 seasons was .325) and leading the league in throwing out runners from center field. He was voted and named to the all-star team every single season and led the Yankees into the World Series ten of those 13 years. But Joe's statistics don't do justice to his gracefulness as an athlete. He made catching a difficult fly ball look easy. He loped like an antelope across the outfield grass, sensing exactly where the ball would drop. He was a smart, focused player with great discipline at bat, which meant he waited for the right pitch before he swung. How else could he have set the record in 1941 for hitting safely in 56 consecutive games? That record still stands.

Although a shy man, Joe DiMaggio was polite to fans. He was also a perfectionist, and he retired after the 1951 season

*Opposite*: Mickey Mantle bashing the ball from the left side of the plate. He had home-run power from both sides.

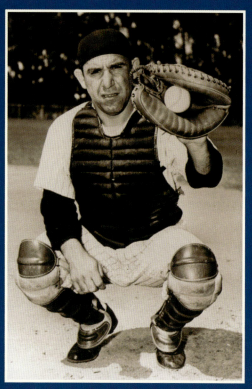

Yogi Berra

Lawrence Peter Berra played for the Yankees from 1946 through 1963. An all-star catcher and a member of the Hall of Fame, he appeared in fourteen World Series. When he retired as a player, he managed both the Yankees and the New York Mets. Yogi is recognized as one of the greatest catchers of all time, but he's just as famous for his wacky sayings:

"Always go to people's funerals. Otherwise they won't go to yours."

"You wouldn't have won if we had beaten you."

because he felt he just wasn't as good as he used to be. He didn't want fans to see anything less than the best. For that same reason, while he would show up at old-timers' games and even would don his old uniform, he would never play. He wanted to be remembered at his best.

Joe was also remembered for having been married to the famous movie star, Marilyn Monroe. Once, after she had returned from a tour to entertain American soldiers at military bases overseas, she told Joe that she had never heard such cheering. He just smiled and said that he had.

If any other Yankees player was destined to hear such cheering, it should have been Mickey Mantle. He was supposed to be the new Joltin' Joe (as DiMaggio was known), if not the new Bambino. The Mick played in the golden age of baseball, the 1950s and 1960s, when the game was not only the national pastime but just about the *only* pastime—pro-football and pro-basketball had yet to make their real impacts in professional sports, and video games, the Internet and X-Games were just science-fiction stories.

Mickey was only 19 years old when he joined the mighty New York Yankees in 1951, DiMaggio's final season. He was bashful and nervous. Originally a shortstop, he was moved to the outfield alongside the great Joe D., the most famous Yankees player since the Babe. The extremely high expectations for him were a heavy weight on his mind, along with the fact that no male member of his family had ever lived past the age of 41.

To look at him, no one would have thought he had a care in the world, this handsome blond with a country-fresh grin. He had muscles in places where most people didn't have places. And even his name made people smile. (There was already an American icon with the initials M. M.: Mickey Mouse.)

Mantle's father, whose name was Elvin (everybody called him Mutt) had named him after the great Philadelphia catcher, Mickey Cochrane. Mutt was determined that little Mickey, born in Spavinaw, Oklahoma, in a two-room shack on a tenant farm, would grow up to be a major leaguer. That had been Mutt's dream for himself, but he'd ended up a lead miner. Every day after work he practiced with Mickey. He had some good ideas, too. He made Mickey learn to bat from both sides of the plate—and Mickey turned out to be one of the best switch-hitters in baseball history.

Mickey was also incredibly strong, which he attributed to his teenage summers working in the lead mines with his dad as a screen ape, a job that required hours of smashing large rocks into small rocks with a sledgehammer. No wonder Mickey developed such powerful wrists, shoulders, arms, and forearms and hit some of the longest homers in history.

But he didn't hit them right away. In fact, he got off to a very shaky start.

Unsure of himself, a country boy out of place in the big city, he went into an immediate slump during his rookie season in 1951. Fans booed him. Manager Casey Stengel sent him down to a minor-league team in Kansas City to regain his confidence and his hitting eye. He played no better there. Mickey called his father and told him that he didn't think he had the talent to play major-league baseball.

To Mickey's surprise, Mutt showed up the next day

"You couldn't keep a conversation going. Everyone was talking too much."

"When you come to a fork in the road, take it."

"That place is so crowded nobody goes there anymore."

"You better cut the pizza into four pieces because I'm not hungry enough to eat six."

"Baseball is 90 percent mental; the other half is physical."

"I knew I was going to take the wrong train, so I left early."

"It ain't over till it's over."

(He also said, "I didn't say half the things I said.")

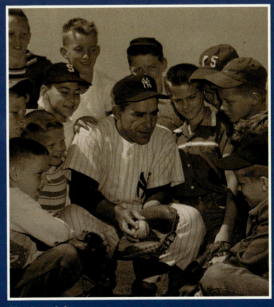

Yogi and fans

was hurting him, so Mickey should try to catch any ball he could get to.

In the second game, the other hot rookie of 1951, Willie Mays, hit a high fly to center. Mickey ran over, but at the last moment, DiMaggio yelled, "I got it!" Mickey stopped short, so he wouldn't run into DiMaggio, and caught his spikes in the rubber cover of a drain hole buried in the grass. His knee popped, and he went down as if shot.

On his way to the doctor the next day, Mickey leaned on his dad for support. Mutt collapsed. They ended up watching the rest of the series in adjoining hospital beds. Mutt was dying from a cancer called Hodgkin's disease. He would be dead before he was 40.

at his Kansas City hotel room and started throwing his son's clothes into his old cardboard suitcase. When Mickey asked his father what he was doing, Mutt said he was taking him home. "Thought I raised a ballplayer," said Mutt. "You ain't nothing but a coward and a quitter."

Mickey begged for one more chance. Both men burst into tears. Mantle went out to the ballpark that afternoon and stroked five hits, including two homers. In August he was brought back up to the Yankees. In the first game of the World Series against the Giants, Mickey started in right field. The great DiMaggio was in center. Manager Stengel told Mickey that DiMaggio's heel

Mickey's knee injury was just the first of various leg injuries that plagued him throughout his 18 years with the Yankees. He never played a game after that without being in pain. As a teenager, Mickey had been diagnosed as having osteomyelitis, an inflammatory disease of the bone. Local doctors in his small Oklahoma town wanted to amputate one of his legs. But Mickey's mother saved it by getting a lawyer to draw up papers transferring Mickey to the charity ward of a major hospital in Oklahoma City, 175 miles away. There, more sophisticated doctors with a new drug—penicillin—brought down his temperature and swelling.

*Above*: Yankees star center fielder Joe DiMaggio.

It's hard to believe that it was only a couple of years later that the switch-hitting strong man began a major-league career in which he hit 536 home runs, batted .300 in ten seasons, and made the American League all-star team 16 times.

Numbers only begin to suggest the hope that sprang forth every time Mantle sauntered to the plate. His power, energy, and youth reflected America in the 1950s. All things were possible when you had infinite resources and the will to win. The United States had led the European forces that defeated Nazi Germany, Italy, and Japan in World War II. It was the first superpower to have the atomic bomb. There was no doubt in the minds of many Americans that they would win the so-called Cold War with the Soviet Union and its Communist allies and dominate the world the way Mickey and the Yankees dominated baseball.

Mickey's golden year was 1956, when he was voted the American League's Most Valuable Player. He won the Triple Crown, batting .353, hitting 52 homers, and driving in 130 runs. The Yankees went on to beat the Dodgers in the World Series. And remember—his legs never stopped hurting him throughout his entire career. Clenching his teeth against the pain, he played as hard as he could. His teammates appreciated his efforts: He was their hero.

Nevertheless, those first ten years of Mickey's career were hard on him. While he was a fun-loving ringleader in the locker room with his teammates, he was shy and frequently rude with fans and sportswriters. The crowd often booed him because he wasn't Babe Ruth or Joe DiMaggio. Mickey didn't become a favorite of the fans until 1961, the year he and Roger Maris chased the Babe's ghost.

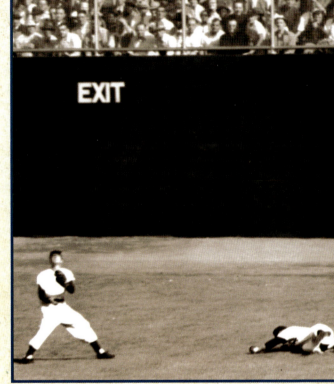

New York was the capital of baseball in those days. The Giants and Dodgers fielded great teams, winning eight National League pennants and two World Series between

*Above*: Mickey Mantle lies hurt as DiMaggio fields a fly ball in the 1951 World Series. Mantle tore up his knee on this play, made during his rookie season.

them. The best were the "subway series" when one of them played against the Yankees. You could always get an argument in the Big Apple over whose center fielder was the best—Mantle, Duke Snider of the Dodgers, or the "Say Hey Kid," Willie Mays.

Many people believe that Willie was not only the best of the three, he was the best all-round ballplayer of all time! His statistics were amazing. He had 3,283 hits, 660 of them home runs. He was the National League Rookie of the Year in 1951, and played in 24 all-star games. He won 12 Gold Gloves and was twice voted the league's Most Valuable Player.

But it was more than the numbers that set Willie apart. He played with an enthusiasm and a sheer joy that filled the ballpark. There was no question that he loved the game, and that made fans feel good. He ran so hard—on the base paths and in the outfield—that he often ran right out from under his cap.

Willie played for the Giants in New York, and then San Francisco, when the team moved after the 1957 season. He ended his career with the New York Mets. (Along the way he became friends with fellow outfielder

Bobby Bonds and godfather to his young son, Barry, who grew up to be another great slugging outfielder, the best of his time.)

Baseball depends on its heroes. While Willie and Mickey were helping to make the game popular in New York, it wasn't doing as well in the rest of the country. In 1948, 21 million fans paid their way into major-league ballparks to see their teams play. By 1952 the number had dropped to 15 million.

The explanation was simple. Americans were on the move. Millions moved out west and to the suburbs. They played golf and went to backyard barbecues.

And then they found a new way to enjoy themselves—television. Even though the first World Series game was televised in 1947, television was still a new toy owned by very few. Ten years later, 75 percent of all American households owned at least one TV set. By 1960 the number had increased to 90 percent. It was a lot easier to sit at home and watch *The Milton Berle Show* or *Father Knows Best* for free in the living room than to go to the ballpark and pay to watch a baseball game.

*Above*: Hall of Famer Duke Snider patrolled center field for the Dodgers at the same time Mickey and Willie Mays played center for the Yankees and Giants, respectively. *Opposite*: New York Giants' Willie Mays making a great outfield catch at the Polo Grounds. Some think that Mays was baseball's best all-around player.

Some baseball owners tried to cash in on television's growing popularity by signing contracts with local television stations to broadcast their games. The results were mixed. Teams in large cities, like New York and Chicago, did well. Ball clubs in smaller cities fared poorly.

Some owners dealt with the decline of baseball's popularity and in their profits in more dramatic fashion. They moved west too. Between 1953 and 1958, five teams relocated: the Boston Braves to Milwaukee, the St. Louis Browns to Baltimore, the Philadelphia Athletics to Kansas City, the New York Giants to San Francisco, and the Brooklyn Dodgers to Los Angeles.

The major leagues also expanded with the organization of brand-new teams. In 1962 the New York Mets joined the Yankees as the other team in New York. Houston got its Colt .45s, and the American League added its own Los Angeles franchise, the Angels. By then, Kansas City had moved to Oakland, California, and different versions of the Washington Senators had relocated to Minnesota and then to Texas! It was more than a little confusing as some teams moved two or three times and others, like the Senators, became new clubs with old names.

In virtually every instance, the move was to the west. The hope was that new teams, playing in new stadiums before new audiences, would bring baseball fans back to the ballpark. It took many years, but it eventually worked out as baseball slowly recaptured its audience.

The audience in New York never left, especially in 1961 when the M&M Boys, what the newspapers called Mickey Mantle and Roger Maris, took over the Yankee Stadium stage. After the Giants and Dodgers left and before the Mets arrived, the Yankees were the only baseball show in town. The show within the show was the race between Mickey and Roger to beat Babe Ruth's record of 60 homers in a single season. Most people thought Mickey would win, that Roger, his pal and roommate,

*Above*: While people cheered for Mantle to break Ruth's record, Roger Maris suffered physically—from the game and from fan abuse.

would act as a "rabbit," the term used for a runner who helps another runner stay on pace. Not that Maris wasn't up to the task. The previous year, his first with the Yankees, he had 141 hits, 39 home runs, 112 RBIs, and won the American League Most Valuable Player award.

The two outfielders were a study in contrasts. The Mick, now a seasoned 10-year veteran, acted like a rock star off the field. Maris was a quiet midwesterner, who had been traded to the Yankees from the Kansas City Athletics before the start of the 1960 season. He was totally unused to the demands of the big-city media, and he felt more and more pressure as the season wore on. One sign of this was that his hair started to fall out.

Mantle started out ahead in the home-run derby, but by August, Maris had taken the lead, hitting 24 home runs in 38 games. As the two closed in on the record, Maris kept to himself.

"I don't want to be Babe Ruth," he told one reporter.

But Maris kept on hitting, even after Mantle left the lineup in mid-September with an abscess on his hip. Finally, on September 26, 1961 in the Yankees' 159th game of the season, Maris tied the Babe's record. Less than a week later, in the Yankees' final game of the season, he set a new record, smacking his 61st home run at Yankee Stadium. A surprisingly small crowd was at the stadium to cheer the new home-run king. In fact, Yankees fans had been lukewarm about the prospect all season long. Many felt that the record should never be broken. Claire Ruth, the Babe's widow, even said so. And if it was to be broken, better by Mantle, a true Yankees player, not by a relative newcomer to the House that Ruth Built.

Baseball Commissioner Ford Frick seemed to agree. He argued that Babe's record should not be wiped away. His line of reasoning was this: In 1927 the baseball season was 154 games long. In 1961, with many more teams, it was 162 games, so Roger had more chances to hit homers than did the Babe. (But if you were looking for differences, remember that the Babe never had to play at night, batting against blazing lights, and he didn't have to travel as much as Roger and current players.)

Years later, Maris admitted to a friend, "It would have been a helluva lot more fun if I had never hit those 61 home runs. All it brought me was headaches."

Roger never really enjoyed being famous. But it worked out well for his old pal, Mickey. People started to feel sorry for him, and then, finally, to like him.

"I became the underdog," said Mickey, years later. "Everywhere I went I got standing ovations."

Those ovations were important to

Mickey, but most important, he said, was the good feeling he got when his teammates hugged him after a home run, when they laughed at his locker-room jokes, when he felt like one of the boys.

"Somebody asked me how I would like to be remembered," he said, "and the first thing I thought of is that I really believe that all the players who played with me liked me."

After he retired, Mantle reflected back on his career. He candidly noted that if he had

> "To cure a batting slump, I took my bat to bed with me. I wanted to know my bat a little better."
> —Richie Ashburn, Hall of Fame outfielder

known he would live as long as he did (and not die like the other Mantle men before the age of 41), "I would have taken much better care of myself."

Long after his playing days were over, Mantle was admitted in 1994 to the Betty Ford Center to be treated for alcoholism. When he came out, he talked about his experiences in hopes of helping others recover from drug and alcohol abuse or, better yet, avoid those ills altogether. He received a liver transplant in 1995, and before he died that year at age 63, he

formed a foundation to raise awareness of the importance of becoming an organ donor.

At the funeral for Mickey, the broadcaster Bob Costas said: "His doctors said he was, in many ways, the most remarkable patient they'd ever seen. His bravery, so stark and real, that even those used to seeing people in dire circumstances were moved by his example. Because of that example, organ donations are up dramatically all across America. A cautionary tale has been honestly told and perhaps will affect some lives for the better."

There were a host of great players during the two decades that Mantle roamed center field for the Yankees. Yet for many fans of the game he is the greatest sports hero of that era. Perhaps it's because of the tremendous baggage he carried—having to replace the incredibly popular superstar Joe DiMaggio and being tagged as "the next Babe Ruth." Or maybe it was the fact that it took him an entire decade of playing hard every day to finally win over the New York fans. Perhaps it's because he had more than five tools and used them all to help his teams win, or because all of his teammates looked up to him, and he played his entire career in pain. And, just maybe, it's because of what he did after his playing days had ended—speaking out against drugs and alcohol and using his own behavior as the example of what not to do. He was determined to leave the world a better place, even at the expense of his reputation.

*Opposite*: During the 1961 season, Roger Maris (*left*) and Mickey Mantle (*right*) look at a telegram sent by fans, encouraging them.

# 6 Hanging Tough

**B**aseball players agree that it takes courage to stand up at the plate as 95-mile-an-hour fast balls whiz past your head. It takes courage to stand your ground at second base as a base runner slides in hard, trying to break up the double play. And it certainly takes courage to go out and play, day after day, when your team is losing and you are in a slump.

But sometimes real courage is about standing up for your rights when the world seems against you and even mocks your principles.

Curt Flood was a very special hero of the game, because he was willing to challenge the way in which major-league baseball had operated for almost a century. He was inspired by the example of Jackie Robinson, who also supported his brave stand.

Flood's 15 big-league seasons, mostly with the St. Louis Cardinals, added up to an excellent career. A superb outfielder, he won seven Gold Gloves and was on three all-star teams. He batted a respectable .293. He wasn't much of a slugger (only 85 homers), but he got on base often and scored a lot of runs. As co-captain, he helped lead his team to a World Series victory in 1967 and to the National League pennant the following year.

His impact on the game, however, was far more significant than his statistics.

Remember the reserve rule, instituted all the way back in A. G. Spalding's day, that prevented baseball players from ever leaving the team that first signed them up? A club could trade, sell, or release a player whenever it wanted, but the player had no power at all over his own life. He could be stuck on a team on which he was being treated poorly or sent to a city far from his home without ever having a say in the matter. Some players thought it was a form of slavery, but they didn't get much sympathy from owners who liked the rule and fans who thought players should be thrilled for the chance to get paid to play baseball.

The reserve rule no longer exists because one player, Curt Flood, stood up and hung tough. Baseball owners and even most sportswriters and fans claimed that the rule was necessary for the game to have stability—otherwise players would just jump

*Opposite*: Curt Flood was an outstanding ballplayer for St. Louis, but is better known for challenging baseball's onerous reserve rule.

## Mascots

The San Diego Chicken

Mascots were common among major-league teams as good luck charms well into the 1930s. Often they were men with physical limitations: dwarfs, hunchbacks, even mentally challenged adults.

Sometimes real animals filled in. In 1909 a New Orleans club had a monkey for a mascot. In 1916 the Chicago Cubs kept Joa the Cubbie Bear in a cage outside of Wrigley Field. And when Marge Schott owned the Cincinnati Reds, a Saint Bernard nicknamed "Schotzie" often took the field.

Schotzie died in 1991. In 1995 the Reds started the season slowly. At Marge's suggestion, the Reds' players rubbed their chests with a bag of Schotzie's hair that she had saved, for good luck. That day they went out and scored nine runs in the last two innings to beat the Mets. That year, they won their division title.

Over the last 30 years, humans dressed up in outlandish animal costumes have become the rage. The

from club to club, looking for a better deal, and the game would collapse the way the old leagues fell apart.

In fact, attendance and interest in baseball has actually increased since the reserve rule was wiped off the books. It all started in October 1969, when Curt Flood refused to be traded from St. Louis to the Philadelphia Phillies. August Busch, the Cardinals owner, had every right to do that. Under the reserve rule, in effect for almost a century, the player's only choice was either to accept what he was offered or refuse to play at all.

Flood made a different choice: He challenged the reserve rule.

In a letter to Baseball Commissioner Bowie Kuhn, Flood demanded his right to be a free agent. "I do not feel that I am a piece of property to be bought and sold irrespective of my wishes," he wrote. "I believe that any system which produces that result violates my basic rights as a citizen and is inconsistent with the laws of the United States. . . ."

He added that although he had received a contract from the Phillies, he should have the right to consider offers from all other major-league clubs. The Phillies' offer was a generous one, but money was not the issue. Flood had sunk roots in St. Louis, raised a family, and begun a second career as a painter.

But it was what he considered baseball's hypocrisy, in the midst of national turmoil over the Vietnam War and the recent assassinations of Martin Luther King Jr. and Robert Kennedy, that truly moved Flood.

"Good men were dying for America and the Constitution," he said. "In the southern part of the

United States we were marching for civil rights . . . and now I found that all of those rights that these great Americans were dying for, I didn't have in my own profession."

When Commissioner Kuhn denied his request, Flood decided to sit out the 1970 baseball season. In 1971 he played for the Washington Senators, and then retired. But he continued to challenge the reserve rule in the courts.

The Major League Baseball Players Association—the players' union—led by its executive director, Marvin Miller, supported his decision, but not until white players asked Flood if his suit was in response to baseball's long history of racial discrimination. Flood was African American.

Coolly, Flood admitted that he believed he had suffered harder times than white players and that "the change in black consciousness in recent years has made me more sensitive to injustice in every area of my life." But he was filing the suit, he said, against a "situation" that was "improper" for *all* players.

Active major-league players did not publicly support Flood. They were afraid that the owners would take revenge on them. Two former players, who had faced discrimination and hard times, Hank Greenburg and Jackie Robinson, did testify at his trial. Robinson said: "Anything that is one-sided is wrong in America. The reserve clause is one-sided in favor of the owners and should be modified to give the player some control over his destiny."

Robinson thought highly of Flood as a principled and courageous man. Years before, when Robinson tried to get active athletes involved in civil rights

San Diego Chicken and the Phillies Phanatic remain the most popular. But there also have been Fred Bird of the Baltimore Orioles, the Seattle Mariners' Moose, and Homer of the Atlantic Braves. For a brief time in the 1980s, the San Francisco Giants had the Crazy Crab, even though the Giants' fans had voted against having a mascot.

Their routines owe much to Al Schacht, who was known as the "Clown Prince of Baseball." A former major-league pitcher and coach, Al took the field in baseball pants and cleats, tuxedo tails, and a top hat. He wore a catcher's mitt almost as big as he was. A star of the vaudeville circuit, Al entertained the fans with sight gags. He pretended to be a nervous pitcher or a boxer being knocked out in slow motion.

The Clown Prince of Baseball did not perform for just one team. After a short career as a pitcher, Schacht became the mascot for all of baseball. He entertained at ballparks for more than 3 decades, including 25 World Series and 18 all-star games.

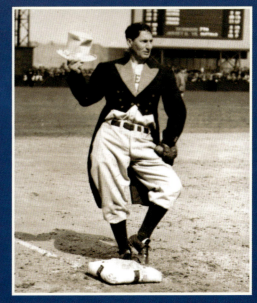

Al Schacht, the Clown Prince of Baseball

demonstrations and fund-raisers, Flood was one of the few who answered his call.

Among those who were not afraid of taking a stand—for civil rights—against apartheid in South Africa, even for Curt Flood, was Jim Bouton, a Yankees pitcher in the 1960s. Nicknamed "Bulldog" for his tenacious style on the mound, Bouton won 21 games in 1963 but is best remembered for *Ball Four*, the controversial bestseller he published in 1970. The book was very funny and good-spirited. But the baseball establishment and many sportswriters complained about it. They said it had four-letter words and showed players in a poor light, being rude to fans, and getting drunk.

But what they were really angry about was the way in which Bouton revealed baseball as a business. There were inside peeks at negotiating sessions between players and executives (the executives always won) and revelations about player salaries. Curt Flood was high-priced at $90,000 a year. Many players were making only $12,000.

During the 3 years it took for Flood's case

to reach the United States Supreme Court, players, sportswriters, and fans began to talk seriously about baseball as a business instead of just a game. Ballplayers needed decent health plans and pensions, just like other workers. Was it fair for owners to shuffle their players like cards, even move the entire team to another city? Bouton's book was as important as Flood's case in provoking the discussion. But it was the case that really scared baseball.

In 1972 Miller organized the first strike by players in both leagues in the game's history. By a vote of 663-10, major-league players decided to stay away from spring training. They didn't return until mid-April, sacrificing more than $1 million in salaries in order to show their solidarity. Most teams ended up playing five fewer games that season, costing owners an estimated $5 million in ticket sales.

Worried about Flood's court case, baseball owners relaxed some of their strict rules in their next contract with the players' union. They allowed a player with ten years in the major leagues and at least five of

*Above*: Baseball Commissioner Bowie Kuhn at a press conference in 1970.

those years with the same club the right to refuse any trade.

They also agreed to permit binding arbitration in contract disputes between a baseball club and a player who had been in the majors at least two years. Binding arbitration meant that both sides to any dispute would make their cases before an independent person. He or she would then decide what salary or other terms were appropriate. Both sides would then have to accept the decision.

So baseball was already instituting change by the time Flood lost his Supreme Court case in a 5-3 vote.

But the decision was not really a defeat. While baseball's exemption from federal antitrust laws was upheld and the reserve rule remained in effect, several justices noted that this privilege was "an aberration" that needed to be corrected, not by the courts but by Congress.

Flood's defeat was about to turn into a huge victory.

At the end of the 1975 season, two pitchers, Dave McNally and Andy Messersmith, made brave by Flood's courage, refused to be traded. The issue, however, was not salary, but the reserve rule itself. McNally, who had spent many years in a Baltimore uniform, had been traded to Montreal. Messersmith pitched for the Los Angeles Dodgers. Both men played in 1975 but refused to sign their contracts. Their lawyers argued that by doing so, they were no longer bound by the reserve rule. Under the new binding arbitration rule, they made their case to a three-person board that voted 2-1 in their favor.

The reserve rule was overturned and baseball changed forever.

Baseball owners cried foul. They went to court to have the decision reversed. When that failed, they took their case to the public.

*Above (from left to right):* Trio of Yankee pitchers. Jim Bouton, Al Downing, and Whitey Ford. Bouton was a bulldog on the mound and a straight-shooter in his tell-all book about baseball.

better deal may have been one reason why it's still America's game. But he suffered for it. He said once: "I am pleased that God made my skin black, but I wish he had made it thicker." Flood was hurt by the indifference to his case shown by his fellow players. But his suffering didn't end there. Pursuing the case cost him the balance of his baseball career as well as the income that would have brought him.

But he never wavered in his principles, a true hero of baseball for fighting injustice and inequality in the game that he loved.

Without the reserve rule, they claimed, baseball would be forever ruined. Players would move from team to team in search of the highest salary. Fan loyalty would be destroyed. Pennants and World Series championships would go to teams with the biggest bankrolls. Baseball would no longer be America's game.

They didn't mention that just that year there had been more than 100 trades between teams, and that in the previous 24 years 18 major-league franchises had been created or moved to a new city, all to make money. And baseball had survived.

Curt Flood's courage in giving players a

*Above*: Andy Messersmith. *Above, right*: Dave McNally. Both men successfully finished Curt Flood's challenge of baseball's reserve rule. *Opposite*: Rachel and Jackie Robinson wait to testify at a congressional hearing about baseball.

#  **7 The Summer of Swat**

In the quarter of a century between Curt Flood's 1970 Supreme Court decision and the great slugfest of 1998, there were seven major conflicts between owners and players over salaries, free agency, and profit-sharing. Seven times either owners or players stopped a baseball season over such disputes. When the players set a strike date of August 12, 1994, owners voted to cancel the remainder of the baseball season. For the first time in its history, there was no World Series.

Baseball fans were upset that greed and big money had taken over their beloved game. They wanted to believe that the problems of the real world had no place in the sanctuary of the Pastime.

No wonder fans felt so good on September 7, 1998, when Big Mac and Sammy strode onto a St. Louis field like cowboy gunfighters in a showdown. But they were carrying wooden bats, not six-shooters, and they were out to destroy a record, not each other or the game.

Big Mac, otherwise known as Mark McGwire, had already hit 60 home runs that season. He needed only one more to tie the single-season record Roger Maris had set in 1961, before either Mark or Sammy were born. Sammy Sosa was only two homers behind Mark, with 58.

While Big Mac and Sammy were in a race to break Maris's record, they were also chasing the ghost of Babe Ruth. Fans had never totally accepted Roger as the "Home Run King." They wanted someone with a bigger, jollier personality, more like the Babe's. Mark and Sammy were friendly guys, and their respect for each other made fans feel good about both of them.

It also made for one of the greatest seasons in baseball history.

McGwire and Sosa were not the only exciting players of that time.

There was Cal Ripken Jr., the Baltimore Orioles' slugger and Gold Glove shortstop who played more games without a day off than any other player in baseball history. Cal appeared in 2,632 consecutive games from May 30, 1982 to September 20, 1998, surpassing the record of 2,130 that Lou Gehrig had set in 1939. Cal seemed like a hardworking, sweaty, lunch-pail kind of guy, who showed up for work even if he wasn't

*Opposite*: Sammy Sosa (*left*) and Mark McGwire (*right*) go head-to-head in their home-run contest during the 1998 season.

## Records That Will Never Be Broken

Ted Williams once said that all he wanted out of life "is that when I walk down the street, folks will say, 'There goes the greatest hitter who ever lived.'"

In 1941, only his third major-league season, "Teddy Ballgame" was already living his dream. Not only did he lead the American League with 37 home runs, he batted .406. No player since has ever hit for a higher average and no one has come close to cracking that magic .400 mark.

That same year, another young ballplayer established another baseball mark that has never been surpassed. On May 15, Joe DiMaggio, the New York Yankees' center fielder, singled in a game against the Chicago White Sox. In each of the next 55 games, Joe got at least one hit. By the time the streak ended after 56 games on July 17 against Cleveland, Joe had smashed the former major-league

Ted Williams

feeling well. Cal Ripken really came to play.

Then there was Roger Clemens. By the Summer of Swat, this hard-throwing right-hander was wrapping up his fifth Cy Young Award as best pitcher in the American League. He had spent 13 seasons with the Boston Red Sox before moving to the Toronto Blue Jays for two seasons. But that was only the beginning. There would be five years with the Yankees, a sixth Cy Young Award, and inclusion in the major-league All-Century Team. And then, in 2004, in the summer of his 42nd birthday, he was a leading pitcher in the National League with the Houston Astros. What was his secret? He worked harder at staying in shape than players half his age.

And there were two superstar outfielders who were also the sons of star outfielders.

Some people thought that Ken Griffey Jr. was not only the most complete ballplayer of his time—he could hit, field, run, and throw with the best in the game—but one of the best of all time. At 30, he was the youngest member of that All-Century Team. But after 11 seasons with the Seattle Mariners as a perennial all-star and Gold Glove winner, Junior, as he's called, was traded to the Cincinnati Reds in 1999 and began to spend more time on the disabled list than on the field. By 2004, as he closed in on 500 homers and a certain spot in the Hall of Fame, Junior seemed to be healthy again. But now he was overshadowed by his long time rival, Barry Bonds.

The son of Bobby Bonds, Barry spent seven years with the Pittsburgh Pirates before joining the San Francisco Giants in 1993. He seemed to get better as he got older, especially as a hitter. And then he exploded in 2001 with 73 home runs, a new baseball record. Perhaps because of his less than friendly personality or the rumors that his newly muscled body had been pumped by steroids, Barry never came close to the popularity of Sammy Sosa or Mark McGwire. But then again, Sammy and Mark's Summer of Swat was a hard act to follow. They not only enchanted baseball fans but captured the imagination of even those Americans who did not ordinarily pay much attention to the game. Everybody could feel good about the friendly rivalry between Sammy and Mark.

The two men seemed so different. Mark was white, red-headed, middle-class. He was nicknamed "Tree," for his size. Mark played all sports, especially golf and baseball, before enrolling at the University of Southern California on a baseball scholarship. He had played on the 1984 United States Olympic baseball team.

Sammy was a dark-skinned Latin American from the poor streets of Consuelo, a small town in the Dominican Republic. As a child, he spent most of his free time helping his widowed mother support the family. He shined shoes and sold orange juice. Like many young Dominicans, he loved baseball. His first glove was made out of milk cartons, and he used a tree limb as a bat. The ball was a taped, rolled-up sock.

Sammy was a skinny, 160-pound 19-year-old, known for his speed, when he signed his first professional major-league baseball contract with the Texas Rangers in 1985.

McGwire was already a giant known for his power when he signed with the Oakland Athletics.

As a major-league rookie in 1987, Big Mac blasted 49 home runs, knocked in 118 runs, and batted .289.

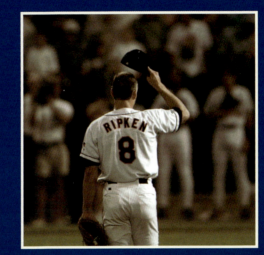

Cal Ripken Jr.

mark of 44 set by Wee Willie Keeler in 1897. In the end, the Yankees Clipper had gotten at least one base hit in 72 of 73 consecutive games!

Lou Gehrig played first base for the New York Yankees when Babe Ruth ruled the baseball world. A gentle giant of a man with his own Hall of Fame credentials, he is best known for just showing up. Between 1925 and the beginning of the 1939 season, the "Iron Horse" played in 2,130 consecutive games. He was sidelined by a deadly illness that took his life in 1941.

Almost a half century later, on September 6, 1995, Cal Ripken Jr., the Baltimore Orioles' shortstop, broke Lou's record by playing in 2,131 consecutive games. Ripken went on to play 2,632 games in a row, before sitting down. His record of consecutive games, along with Joe D.'s 56-game hitting streak, and Ted Williams's single-season .406 batting average are three marks that just may stand forever.

each season. The stage was set for the Summer of Swat.

Baseball, we know, has not always been about the home run. But when Babe Ruth hit 60 home runs in 1927, he changed the game forever. Fans flocked to the ballpark to witness the big bang and to hear the thunderous thwack of wood on horsehide. They came to watch the majestic arc of towering fly balls as they headed out of the ballpark.

He was a unanimous choice for Rookie of the Year.

Sammy didn't join the Rangers until 1989. His rookie season was not special. He batted .238 and hit only one home run in 84 at bats before being traded to the Chicago White Sox.

Over the next decade, both players had their ups and downs. Even though he was often out of the lineup with chronic back injuries, McGwire, with his big bat, still helped the Athletics reach three and win one World Series. But the A's lost confidence in his future and traded him to the St. Louis Cardinals in 1997.

Sosa struggled with the White Sox before they traded him to their crosstown rivals, the Chicago Cubs, in 1992. By then a mature, muscled man, he flourished. From 1993 to 1998, he averaged more than 39 home runs and almost 110 runs batted in

Mark McGwire felt the same way. "Ever since I was a kid," he said, "what do you go to the ballpark for? You go to the ballpark to see somebody hit a home run or somebody throw a ball at close to 100 miles an hour. That was the exciting thing when I was a kid, and I think it still is."

A global audience plugged in by television and the Internet couldn't have agreed more as they watched Sammy and Mark battle each other and chase the records of Roger and the Babe.

After hitting 58 home runs in 1997 and signing a three-year, multimillion-dollar contract with the Cardinals, McGwire was ready. He began the season with a grand-slam home run on opening day, then hit a homer in each of the next three games. Sammy started slowly, hitting only nine

*Above*: Cal Ripken Jr. holds the major-league record for most consecutive games played.

home runs to Mark's 24 by May 24. But then he went on a hot streak, belting 21 home runs over the next 30 days. McGwire kept pace. By midseason's all-star game break, Big Mac had 37, the second player to reach that total in a half-season's play. The race was on.

On August 19, Sammy's Cubs and Mac's Cards met at Chicago's Wrigley Field. Each slugger had 47 home runs. Sammy broke the tie in the fifth inning. Three innings later, Mark tied the game with a solo blast of his own. Then,

in the tenth inning, he hit another home run to win the game.

Every day, Americans became increasingly captivated both by the chase and by the growing friendship the two men showed toward each other as they challenged baseball history. Sportswriters couldn't remember the last time two rivals were so fiercely competitive yet so respectful. The fact that one was black and one was white wasn't lost on fans; after all, baseball had been integrated for only 50 years.

As they entered the last month of the season, they were tied again at 55 homers apiece. A week later, Big Mac had 60, tying the Babe's old record, and Sammy stood at 58. On September 7, they met head-on in St. Louis. Roger Maris's children were in the stands. McGwire delivered, hitting number 61. The stadium erupted, and the game was delayed for 11 minutes. Mark's son, serving as the Cardinals' batboy, greeted his father at home plate. Mark then went into the stands to hug the Maris family. Sammy trotted in from right field to congratulate his friend. Fans cried.

The next night the Cubs and Cards met again. Before a national TV audience, Mark hit number 62. The uproar was even greater. As he crossed home plate, Mark pointed to the sky, in tribute to Maris, who had died in

*Above*: Mark McGwire was a star before he entered major-league baseball and was Rookie of the Year in his first season.

1985. Sammy Sosa greeted Mark with another bear hug.

The race was not yet over. Sammy went on a batting binge. Five days later, he tied McGwire, hitting his 62nd home run before a delirious hometown crowd. He ended the season with 66 home runs and was named the National League's Most Valuable Player for his efforts.

But Mark hadn't cooled off. He belted seven more homers, including two in the last game of the season to establish a new major-league record of 70 home runs in a season.

The Summer of Swat made baseball fans feel good about the game and its history.

> **"I talked to the ball a lot of times in my career. I yelled, 'Go foul. Go foul.'"**
> —Lefty Gomez, Yankee pitcher

Babe Ruth, the man who made the home run the signature of the sport, was back in the headlines again, his ghostly hands on the broad shoulders of two good-guy sluggers. McGwire donated $1 million to the Mark McGwire Foundation for Children, which supports agencies that work with child-abuse victims. Sosa played a major financial and inspirational role in helping the people of the Dominican Republic recover from Hurricane George. He also established the Sammy Sosa Charitable Foundation to further the education and health of children there.

The rosy glow of that magical summer lasted for seven years before it began to fade in the harsh spotlight of grand-jury investigations, congressional hearings, and accusations of performance-enhancing drug use in newspapers, books, and on the

*Above*: Sammy Sosa hits another one during the "Summer of Swat."

bulk up for big bucks. In doing so, they risk damaging their health. They also endanger the health of young fans who try to emulate their heroes.

But the memory of that summer was less about dollars and drugs than about the warmth and friendship that two men showed each other as they fiercely competed for a great prize. They proved it was possible to be both a gladiator and a humane person.

It was a powerful lesson. Baseball had been good to Sammy and Mark, and baseball was still good for America. Two strong men from different countries with different languages—one black, one white, one born poor, the other middle-class—showed the world how to be rivals, friends, and heroes.

Internet. Mark and Sammy were among the players called to Washington, D.C., in 2005. Sammy denied ever using steroids. Mark, looking far less muscular than in his dinger days, avoided answering by saying, "I'm not here to talk about the past." Fans were disappointed.

The controversy pointed out a crisis that baseball and other professional sports have helped create. The huge salaries of professional athletes and the possibilities for even bigger money from commercial endorsements have encouraged many of them to

*Above*: Sosa congratulates McGwire on breaking Roger Maris's home-run record. *Above, right*: After celebrating with Sosa, McGwire ran over to the stands to hug Maris's son.

# 8 The Planet's Game?

When Ichiro Suzuki left his team, the Orix Blue Wave of Kobe, Japan, to join the Seattle Mariners for the 2001 season, he was followed by dozens of Japanese reporters and TV crews, as well as the doubts of many American fans. Could the little guy (he was 5' 9", 160 pounds) stand up to American pitching? Japanese players had been on major-leagues rosters since 1964, but they were all pitchers. Ichiro was the first position player—a right fielder— and although he was one of the best players in Japanese baseball history, many Americans wondered if he could make it in the "real" major leagues.

Ichiro was 27 at the time, which is old for a rookie. But he had already played nine years in the Japanese major leagues, where he had won seven batting titles in a row and seven consecutive Gold Gloves for his fielding. He had led the Orix Blue Wave to two Pacific League titles and a national championship.

Seattle paid Orix $13 million for the right to negotiate with Ichiro, then paid him $14 million for three years. It turned out to be a bargain.

Ichiro batted .350 and stole 56 bases, only the second player in history to lead the majors in both categories (Jackie Robinson did it in 1949). He turned right field into a dead zone for fly balls, and with his powerful arm, threw out eight runners, even assisting on two double plays. It was no surprise when he was voted the American League Rookie of the Year and Most Valuable Player, only the second player in history to win both awards in the same year (Fred Lynn did it in 1975).

Suzuki was friendly and unassuming. During spring training, he told a reporter for the *Seattle Post-Intelligencer* that he was trying to learn one word of English every day. "The only problem," he said, "is that I learn a word, but I go to bed and by the time I wake up, I've forgotten it, so the next day I have to start over."

When the reporter asked what word he had learned today, Ichiro showed his sense of humor, saying, "It was a bad word so I can't say what it was."

Ichiro's great success was no surprise to people who had been watching baseball spread throughout the world. While Japan

*Opposite*: Seattle Mariners' Ichiro Suzuki was baseball's first Japanese superstar, but far from its last.

## Baseball Nicknames

### THE "SAY HEY KID"

Willie Mays (1951–1973, New York/San Francisco Giants, New York Mets) According to sportswriter Barney Kremenko, Mays was a quiet, shy ballplayer who would occasionally yell out, "Say who!" "Say where!" and "Say hey!" Kremenko called him the "Say Hey Kid" in a newspaper column, and it stuck.

### "OIL CAN"

Dennis Boyd (1982–1991, Boston Red Sox, Montreal Expos, Texas Rangers) Dennis once told an interviewer that when he drank a beverage to refresh himself, it went down so well that it was like drinking a can of oil.

Oil Can Boyd

has been an especially baseball-crazed nation—the year before Ichiro arrived, the New York Mets and the Chicago Cubs actually opened the National League season in Tokyo—Latin America has also become an amazing breeding ground for superstars and baseball heroes.

On the opening day of the 2003 baseball season, 230 players—almost 28 percent of all major leaguers—had been born outside of the United States mainland. Of these, 197 came from either Puerto Rico or Latin America. The Dominican Republic topped the list with 79, led by superstar outfielders Sammy Sosa and Manny Ramirez. Shortstop (and later Yankees third baseman) Alex Rodriguez, who was considered the best player in the game at that time, was born in New York to Dominican parents.

There will be even more Latin stars in the years to come. Of the more than 6,000 players signed to minor-league contracts in 2003, more than 2,500 were Latin! The increase in the number of Latin ballplayers in American major and minor leagues did not happen by accident. As the major leagues added new franchises in the 1980s and 1990s, they searched for new talent. They sent scouts to Latin America to find ballplayers. Ever since American sailors introduced baseball to Cuba in the 1860s, the game has spread throughout Latin America. (The first recorded Latin ballplayer here was Esteban Bellan of Cuba, who played for the Troy Haymakers in 1871.)

The Los Angeles Dodgers and the Toronto Blue Jays were the first teams to build baseball academies to train promising Dominican youngsters. Today, major-league baseball teams pay the Dominican Republic $14 million for the right to run 30 such schools, where the only subject taught is baseball.

Such schools might sound tempting, but critics rightfully argue that they fill young boys with false dreams. Only a very small percentage of the young players have a chance of making it in the United States. And by attending the academy they are foregoing a proper public school education. Still, these schools attract boys as young as ten years old, who dream of becoming the next Sammy Sosa.

The first great Latin ballplayer was a naturalized American citizen, Roberto Clemente of Puerto Rico. In 1955, at the age of 20, he joined the Pittsburgh Pirates. Over the next 18 years, he emerged as one of baseball's all-time great players. He batted over .300 in 13 seasons. He was one of only a handful of players to amass over 3,000 career hits. He led the National League in batting four times and made 14 all-star times. He won 12 Gold Gloves as a right-fielder and won the league's Most Valuable Player award in 1966. Twice he led the Pirates to World Series victories—in l960 and again in 1971.

Like African-American baseball players, Clemente often faced discrimination because of his skin color. Because his English was sometimes hard to understand early in his career, there were misunderstandings with sportswriters. But all respected his talent and determination as a player. On July 24, 1970, the Pittsburgh Pirates celebrated his achievements with Roberto Clemente Night. He was the first Latin player to be so honored by a major-league team. Surrounded by his parents and his family, Roberto received a scroll of paper signed by 300,000 Puerto Ricans, wishing him well.

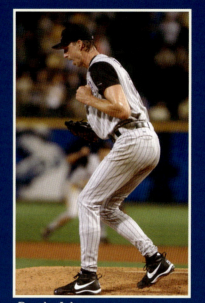
Randy Johnson

**THE "BIG UNIT"**
Randy Johnson (1988–present, Montreal Expos, Seattle Mariners, Houston Astros, Arizona Diamondbacks)

Making his major-league debut for the Expos, teammate Tim Raines saw the 6'10" Johnson step onto the mound and said, "That's one big unit."

**THE "HUMAN RAIN DELAY"**
Mike Hargrove (1974–1985, Texas Rangers, Cleveland Indians)

As a first baseman and designated hitter, Hargrove had a routine at bat between pitches that took close to a half a minute until he was ready for the next pitch. When a baseball game is stopped by a storm, the wait for the weather to pass is called a "rain delay." A writer in Toronto thought that fit and gave Hargrove the nickname.

There was more to Roberto, however. His heart was even bigger than his talent. In late December 1972, when he heard about the earthquake in Managua, Nicaragua, he quickly organized a collection of food and medicine, and hired an airplane to deliver them. It was a rickety old plane, but Roberto insisted on making the trip to be sure the relief supplies reached the people who needed them. They never made it. A few miles after takeoff from Puerto Rico, on New Year's Eve, the plane crashed into the sea. His body was never recovered. Roberto was 38.

Major-league baseball honored Roberto by electing him immediately into Baseball's Hall of Fame, the first Latin player honored. At the induction ceremony at Cooperstown, New York, the baseball commissioner said that Clemente's "marvelous playing skills rank him among the truly elite. And what a wonderfully good man." Clemente was an inspiration for young Latins in a way that has become familiar in America. Ballplayers from each new ethnic wave that enriches the game become role models for young people who have emigrated here and would like to be seen—and treated— as Americans. What better way to start than to play America's game? Around the turn of the twentieth century, the English names that had dominated baseball were replaced by players with Irish names— Kelly, O'Rourke, Delehanty, McGraw. Then came German names— Wagner, Ruth, Gehrig, Hubbell; followed by Italian names—Lazzeri, Crosetti, DiMaggio. There were Jewish ballplayers too: Hank Greenberg, Sandy Koufax, Al Rosen, Sid Gordon, Ken Holtzman, and Moe Berg, the catcher who was better known as an

*Above*: Cuban-born star Orlando "El Duque" Hernandez is one of the great Latin pitchers. *Opposite*: Perhaps the greatest Latin ballplayer who ever lived, Roberto Clemente was known for what he did off the field as much as for what he did on it.

career with the Detroit Tigers. A tall, husky first baseman and outfielder, he played regularly from 1933 through 1947, with three years off during World War II. He was a captain in the U.S. Air Corps and flew on bombing raids over Tokyo. In 1938 he hit 58 homers, only two short of Babe Ruth's famous 60-homer record (which lasted from 1927 to 1961).

Sandy Koufax was only a so-so left-handed pitcher when he first started playing in 1955 with his hometown Brooklyn Dodgers. He was 19 years old and a late bloomer. By the time the Dodgers were established in Los Angeles, Koufax was on his way to becoming one of the greatest left-handers in history, frequently leading the league in strikeouts and earned run average. He was

American spy. Berg became an officer in the Office of Strategic Services in 1943, the year after he retired from baseball. He was only a back-up catcher, but served his country well in World War II. The Jewish player who got the most publicity in his time was one of the first, Andy Cohen, a second baseman from Texas who joined the Giants in 1926. Jewish immigrants packed the stands to cheer Andy. His career lasted only three years, but made many Jewish immigrants feel less like outsiders in a new land.

Hammerin' Hank Greenberg, a Hall of Fame home run hitter, spent most of his

*Above*: Youngsters in the Dominican Republic can go to baseball schools run by the major leagues. *Above, right*: At another baseball academy in the Dominican Republic, the stuffing from a pillow served as third base during a game.

a three-time Cy Young Award winner as best pitcher in Major League Baseball. He was the first pitcher with four no-hitters, and he pitched a perfect game. An exceptionally hard thrower, Koufax pitched through his last three seasons in pain, and retired after the 1966 World Series, after 12 years in the majors. He is admired among Jews and religious people in general for an act of principle: He chose not to pitch the first game of the 1965 World Series because it fell on Yom Kippur, the holiest of Jewish holidays. Koufax was not deeply devout, but he did feel he should spend that day in synagogue. The Dodgers went on to triumph in that series against the Minnesota Twins, with Koufax pitching, and winning the fifth and seventh games.

During all this time, the Japanese were playing baseball. It is generally thought that the game was introduced there in 1873, at what is now Tokyo University. The first professional Japanese team was created in 1934. Today, there are two major leagues: the Central and the Pacific, each with six teams. Although most of their players are Japanese, a certain number of foreigners, mostly Americans, are allowed to play.

Although the rules of the game are basically the same as American rules, Japanese baseball tends to rely less on home runs

*Above*: Sandy Koufax and catcher John Roseboro celebrate after Koufax pitched the Dodgers to victory over the Yankees in the 1963 World Series.

runs in a 22-year career for the Tokyo Giants between 1959 and 1980. Naturally he is called the Babe Ruth of Japan.

The first Japanese player to play in the American major leagues was a pitcher, Masanori Murakami. He played for the San Francisco Giants in 1964 and 1965. In 1995 pitcher Hideo Nomo of the L.A. Dodgers was voted Rookie of the Year.

In 2003 the most consistent player on the World Series–bound New York Yankee team was outfielder Hideki Matsui, one of 11 Japanese ballplayers on major-league opening-day rosters. Following Ichiro's path, he was part of the new wave of Japanese position players in America—with a difference. Hideki was a home-run slugger. He played in every single Yankees game—a major-league record for a rookie —and made the all-star team. In 2004 Hideki was called the most famous person in Japan. He was idolized by millions of fans, young and old, and his success was seen

than on walks, sacrifice flies, and base hits. (It's more like the small ball of Ty Cobb than the slugging of Babe Ruth and Barry Bonds.) Japanese players practice bunting for hours, and are famous for hard work and good fundamental skills. Nevertheless the most celebrated of all Japanese players was Sadaharu Oh, a first baseman who slugged 868 home-

*Above*: Tigers' star Hank Greenberg catches a low fly ball during spring training in 1940.

as an inspiration for his entire nation.

At 6'2" and 210 pounds, Hideki is big for a Japanese player. It was while he was leading his high-school team into the national championships that he got his nickname, both for his size and his monster homers: "Godzilla." The nickname reminded old-time Yankees fans of the slugging outfielder of the 1940s, King Kong Keller.

The Yankees' Godzilla played center field 50 years after King Kong did, in the same outfield made famous by the Bambino, Joltin' Joe, the Mick, Reggie Jackson, and Bernie Williams—players of German, Italian, English, African, and Puerto Rican ancestry, who shared the ability to win a game with a swing of their bats.

One of them, the brash and funny Reggie Jackson, called himself "the straw that stirs the drink." That was his way of saying that he made things happen. And he did. A Hall of Fame slugger, he became known as "Mr. October" for his hot hitting in the World Series. In 1977 he became the first player since Babe Ruth to hit three homers in one World Series game.

A quarter-century later, the graceful Bernie Williams was the star of the Yankees outfield. A dark-skinned Puerto Rican, soft-spoken, and humble, Williams was a superb fielder and slugger, who also played classical guitar.

Maybe the next monster talent in the outfield who will make things happen will come from China. In 2004 Sun Ling-feng played center field for the Beijing Tigers, one of four new professional teams in the country with the world's largest population. The Chinese government is supporting the league and hopes to field a national team to play in the 2008 Olympics, which will be held in China.

The first Chinese baseball player to succeed in the major leagues will become a national hero in China and a role model to Chinese-American youth. In the same way, all foreign-born baseball stars are heroes for youngsters from their cultural backgrounds, who are striving to make it here in America.

*Above*: Reggie Jackson was always at his home run–hitting best in the playoffs and World Series games.

# 9 Next Season

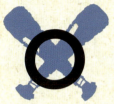

Over the past century, much has changed about the game of baseball. The equipment, for instance, has changed dramatically. Baseballs, once handmade, are now produced by machines that can wrap the ball's interior material so tight that balls are livelier, bounce higher, and travel farther than ever before. Fielders' gloves are the best ever made, allowing for catches that smaller gloves could not make. Even sunglasses have improved, so that fielders don't have to fight sun glare as they chase fly balls. When American League umpires changed from outside chest protectors to new, stronger

inside protectors, it allowed them to get lower in their stance behind the catcher. This brought an end to the "high strike" in the American League and introduced the "low strike." Batters had to adjust.

The players themselves are physically superior now, due to everything from better diet, to better conditioning, to more information about the body and how it functions. Players get better instruction, at every level of play. Players can also take advantage of new technology. They can have tapes made of themselves as they play, and then watch them later to see what they are doing right and what needs to be improved or corrected in the way they swing, run, or approach a pitcher at the plate.

The major-league schedule has been expanded and more games are played now during the season and in the postseason play-offs. Rosters have also expanded over the years, allowing for more specialty players, such as middle-inning relief pitchers, pinch-hitters and

*Opposite, clockwise*: This ball, now in the Baseball Hall of Fame, was used in a nineteenth-century game. Infielder's glove from the early part of the twentieth century. Fielders' gloves from the 1880s. A modern baseball factory uses machines to create more tightly wound and wrapped baseballs. *Above*: Modern sunglasses cut glare better than ever before.

## Pete Rose: You Decide

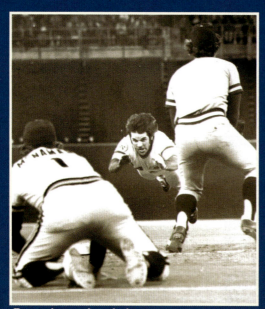

Rose always hustled

Pete Rose is probably the most controversial player in the history of the game. On his record as a hitter, he should be in the Hall of Fame. But because he bet on baseball games, he was banned from baseball and kept out of the Hall.

Some people will probably wonder why he's even mentioned in this book about heroes. What do you think? Was his skill and intensity enough to qualify him as a hero of the game, despite his flaws as a person?

In talent, he was the closest player to Ty Cobb that baseball had seen since the Georgia Peach himself. Except that Pete was known as a nice guy who didn't even drink or smoke.

In 1984, Rose became player-manager of the Reds. Next season he broke Cobb's career-hit record of 4,191. By the time he retired as a player in 1985, Pete had collected more hits

designated hitters, and defensive specialists.

Most games are played at night now, whereas a century ago all games were played during the day. And most games are now routinely broadcast on television. The deal that Major League Baseball has with the television networks includes "TV minutes" for commercials to be broadcast between innings. This has added length to the average baseball game and slowed down the pace. Again, the players have had to adjust. Free agency has also had a dramatic impact on the game. Players change teams more frequently, and proven players from foreign countries are paid to come over here and perform. And that's because the economics of the game have changed. A few baseball franchises are now worth half a billion dollars or more.

So many of the aspects of the game have changed, yet the basic elements remain the same. Three strikes is an out (unless the catcher drops the third strike and the batter beats his throw to first base). Four balls is still a walk. The bases are still 90 feet from one another, and the pitcher's mound is still 60'6" from home plate, which remains 17 inches across. There are still nine position players in the field, and the game ends after the home team's last at-bat—whether it's in the ninth inning or extra innings. If a pitcher retires 27 batters in a row, that is still a perfect game. If a player's career includes 500 home runs or more, or if a pitcher's includes 300 wins or more, they will likely be voted into the Baseball Hall of Fame.

Something else that will not change as baseball moves along in the twenty-first century is how we will define its heroes. The next generation of heroes will be players who show respect for the game, their teammates, and the fans. They will be players who were in the right place at the right time to do extraordinary things within the confines of an ordinary game. They will be players who break new ground in the game, the effects of which will ripple throughout society at large. They will be players who love the game and make their teams better. They will be a joy to watch and will show us how the game is best played. They will allow us to get out of ourselves and enjoy an athletic competition that is a pure team sport—each man plays his part, and together all obstacles can be overcome. They will be players who will dare to be great and not fear failure, even though their jobs are performed in public for the entire world to see.

All of the players mentioned and highlighted in this book knew what it took to be winners in a team sport. Each and every one of them would do just fine in today's—and tomorrow's—game. As noted earlier, Jackie Robinson stole home a total of 19 times during the course of his career. No one has ever done anything like that since, and probably no one ever will. But that is not what made him one of the heroes of the game. As Hank Aaron once said, "Jackie gave us our dreams." He was speaking specifically about African Americans, but it applies in a broader sense as well.

Jackie Robinson was the heart and the soul of the Brooklyn Dodgers. But he was much more than that. He was Brooklyn's representative to the world, one of whom Brooklyn was infinitely proud. Because of the way he played; because of how he conducted himself off the field. Because he insisted on being treated no

(4,256), been to bat more times (14,053), played in more games (3,562), and had more 200 hit seasons (10) than anyone in major-league history. Altogether he held 34 major-league and National League records!

Many people in and out of baseball knew that he liked to bet on the horses. But in 1989, after extensive investigations, the baseball commissioner, A. Bartlett Giamatti, accused Rose of betting on baseball. Despite what appeared to be overwhelming evidence, Rose denied the charge. Giamatti responded by banning Pete Rose from baseball for life. Ever since then, baseball fans and sportswriters have debated whether or not Rose should be denied his place in the Baseball Hall of Fame.

In 2004 Rose finally admitted that he had bet on the game he loved, although never against his own team. Some wondered if he was truly sorry. Or was this just another hustle—a last gasp attempt to win reinstatement, and then attainment of the one prize that has eluded him?

Would you vote for or against Pete?

Rose denied gambling.

also gave credibility to Latin ballplayers and ensured their legitimacy as stars of the game. His death while trying to help the earthquake victims in Nicaragua was a tragedy. But the way he lived his life made baseball fans proud that he had played the game.

These are the attributes that can raise a ballplayer's status from star to hero. Their actions allow us to feel better about ourselves and about our society. They show us the joy and excitement that can come from teamwork and competition. Over the course of a century, they helped raise baseball from a game to the national pastime and, more recently, an international pastime. They represent to us the best that people can aspire to be. In that sense, all of baseball's heroes give us our dreams.

differently from others both on and off the field.

Babe Ruth also "gave us our dreams." In a time when the average American was a "wage slave" and told to "keep your nose to the grindstone," Ruth allowed people to forget their daily worries, their jobs, and their debts. His lowly origins and soaring success seemed to say that all things were possible in America, that dreams of a better life through hard work could come true.

Roberto Clemente was a gentleman and a superstar player, whose presence made the Pittsburgh Pirates a much better team. He

*Above and right*: Roberto Clemente makes a spectacular running catch, then tips his cap to the appreciative fans. *Opposite, clockwise*: They "gave us our dreams": Jackie Robinson, Roberto Clemente, and Babe Ruth.

# GLOSSARY

**All-Star Game**—Once a year the best players in each league (as voted by the fans and the managers of each team) play one another in one game in the middle of the season.

**Amateur team**—A recreational group that gets together to play for free and for the fun of the game.

**American League**—Started in 1900 with just six teams, the American League now consists of fourteen baseball teams. It was organized later than the National League, and is sometimes called the "junior circuit" because of that. The sole difference with the National League is the implementation of the designated hitter rule. In the American League, pitchers are not required to bat. Instead another player called the "designated hitter" bats in his place.

**Baseball academies**—A group of so-called schools in many South American, Caribbean, and Asian countries that teach baseball to young people and train them for careers in playing the game. Some are sponsored by major-league baseball teams, while others are subsidized by the country's government.

**National Baseball Hall of Fame**—The organization in Cooperstown, New York, that honors former players, managers, club executives, and umpires. Every year the Baseball Writers Association of America votes to induct into the Hall new members who had outstanding careers in the game.

**Clothesline peg**—A straight, hard throw from an outfielder to an infielder that doesn't bounce. Also referred to as "a frozen clothesline."

**Cricket**—A British game in which a bowler takes the place of the pitcher and throws a ball at wickets. A batsman gets his team runs by defending the wickets with his bat, and is out if the wickets are hit or he flies out. This is considered by many to be the true precursor to baseball.

**Cy Young Award**—An honor given annually by the Baseball Writers Association of America in which they vote for the best pitcher in each league. It is named after Hall of Fame pitcher Cy Young, who is considered to be one of the best pitchers to ever play the game.

**Expansion team**—A new major-league baseball club in either league. In the modern age of baseball, an expansion team is composed of players from other teams who are chosen by the new club in a special "expansion draft."

**Extra base hit**—A double, triple, or home run.

**Golden Glove**—An annual award sponsored by Rawlings, given out to the best fielder at each position in each league, including pitchers. This usually goes to the player who has made the least number of errors at his position.

**Grand slam**—A home-run hit when there are base runners on first, second, and third bases.

**National League**—The original baseball league that was started in 1876, which now has sixteen teams. Because it came before the American League, the National League is known as the "senior circuit."

**The Pennant**—Traditionally, at the start of each new season, the teams that won their league championships the previous year are allowed to raise a flag, or pennant, in their stadium that proclaims their championship from the year before. Winning the pennant means winning a league championship.

**Perfect game**—A rare event in which a pitcher does not allow the opposing team a single base runner during the course of a complete game.

**Playoffs**—The postseason period of baseball. In each league, the three division leaders plus one "wild card" team (which has the best record of the nondivision winners), play one another to decide who plays in the World Series. The first round is a best-of-five series called the "Divisional Play-off." The second round is a best-of-seven series called the "Championship Series." The winners of the first two play-off rounds in each league then meet in the World Series, which is also a best-of-seven.

**RBI**—Run Batted In. When a player comes to bat with one or more men on base who subsequently score because of something the batter has done, whether it is a hit, a walk, or a sacrifice fly. The batter is credited with the run or runs that score because of his at-bat.

**Reserve rule**—The clause in baseball's original constitution stating that a player must stay with his team unless he is bought by another team or traded by his original team. This prevented players from choosing which team they would play for.

**Retired number**—To honor a player, coach, or manager, a team may remove from their roster the number worn by that person during his career. The number is said to be "retired." In 1997 Major League Baseball retired Jackie Robinson's number, 42, in perpetuity. This means it will never be worn by another baseball player.

**Rookie**—A player in his first full year in the major leagues.

**Round-tripper**—A nickname for a home run, because after hitting one, the batter makes a complete trip around the bases.

**Sacrifice fly**—A fly ball that is caught for an out but allows for a runner on base to advance after the out has been called.

**Segregation**—A discredited and discarded social and political policy of separating people based on the color of their skin. In baseball this policy was enforced by the owners of the teams until 1947, when Brooklyn Dodgers' owner Branch Rickey hired Jackie Robinson to play on his previously all-white team.

**Semipro team**—A franchise that is part of a regional or independent league in which the players are paid but don't play baseball as a full-time job.

**Slugger**—Nickname given to a player who is known for his ability to hit home runs and extra base hits.

**Steroids**—Hormones that stimulate organ and muscle growth in the human body. Some are made naturally by the body, while others are created in laboratories. The latter are called "synthetic steroids." The use of synthetic steroids is forbidden in baseball and all professional sports, as it gives the user an unfair advantage over all other players. It is a banned substance, and any player discovered to be using it is subject to stiff fines and other penalties.

**Subway Series**—Term coined in the 1940s for World Series that were played between the New York Yankees and either the New York Giants or the Brooklyn Dodgers. Because the teams were all in the same city, fans could go from one team's ballpark to the other by taking public transportation, which in New York meant taking the subway.

**Spring training**—The period of time, usually about one month, before the opening day of the baseball season in which every team trains in either Florida or Arizona and plays exhibition games to tune up for the coming season.

**Stoole ball**—A predecessor to the game cricket in which a stool is set upon the ground and a player take turns attempting to hit it with a ball, while a defenseman tries to prevent the ball from hitting it with his hands.

**Switch-hitter**—A batter who can hit both left-handed and right-handed.

## FURTHER READING and ONLINE RESOURCES

### FICTION

*Bang the Drum Slowly* by Mark Harris
*The Bingo Long Traveling All-Stars and Motor
    Kings* by William Brashler
*The Great American Novel,* by Philip Roth
*Hoopla,* by Harry Stein
*The Natural* by Bernard Malamud
*The Rabbi of Swat,* by Peter Levine
*Shoeless Joe,* by W. P. Kinsella
*The Universal Baseball Association, Inc.,* by Robert
    Coover
*You Know Me, Al,* by Ring Lardner

### NONFICTION

*1,001 Baseball Questions Your Friends Can't Answer*
    by Dom Forker
*Ball Four* by Jim Bouton
*The Ballpark Book: A Journey Through the Fields of
    Baseball Magic* by Rod Smith
*Fair Ball: A Fan's Case for Baseball* by Bob Costas
*Game Time: A Baseball Companion* by Roger Angell
*Great Moments in Baseball History* by Matt
    Christopher
*Total Baseball: The Ultimate Baseball Encyclopedia
    (Total Baseball)* by John Thorn, et al.
*Why is the Foul Pole Fair? (Or Answers to the
    Baseball Questions Your Dad Hoped You Wouldn't
    Ask)* by Vince Staten
*The Yogi Book: "I Really Didn't Say Everything I
    Said"* by Yogi Berra

### WEB SITES

**The Baseball Almanac**
www.baseball-almanac.com
One of the most comprehensive sites to find
information about players, dates and historical
facts.

**Major League Baseball's Official Web site**
www.mlb.com
Find out all 30 teams' schedules, buy tickets, or
even watch games online with up-to-the-minute
score updates.

**National Baseball Hall of Fame and Museum**
www.baseballhalloffame.org
The official site for Cooperstown. You can plan
your visit to upstate New York or research lists
and stats for inductees.

**Baseball Prospectus**
www.baseballprospectus.com/
If you're looking for in-depth player analysis with
statistics, both simple and complicated, this is the
authority.

**Black Baseball's Negro Baseball Leagues**
www.blackbaseball.com/
A website devoted solely to the history and
current studies of the Negro Leagues.

**Baseball Notebook**
www.baseballnotebook.com/
A crack team of writers who deal with fantasy
baseball and the effect the real game has on
fantasy general managers.

**ESPN.com**
espn.go.com
Click on the MLB link, and you'll find a lineup of
today's best sportswriters, from Peter Gammons
to Buster Olney.

**Net Shrine**
www.netshrine.com
A site that celebrates the all-time greats of the
game and even the players who made a small
impact in their own time that aren't necessarily
Hall of Famers.

**BaseballParks.com**
www.baseballparks.com/
Everything you ever wanted to know about minor
league and major-league parks is here.

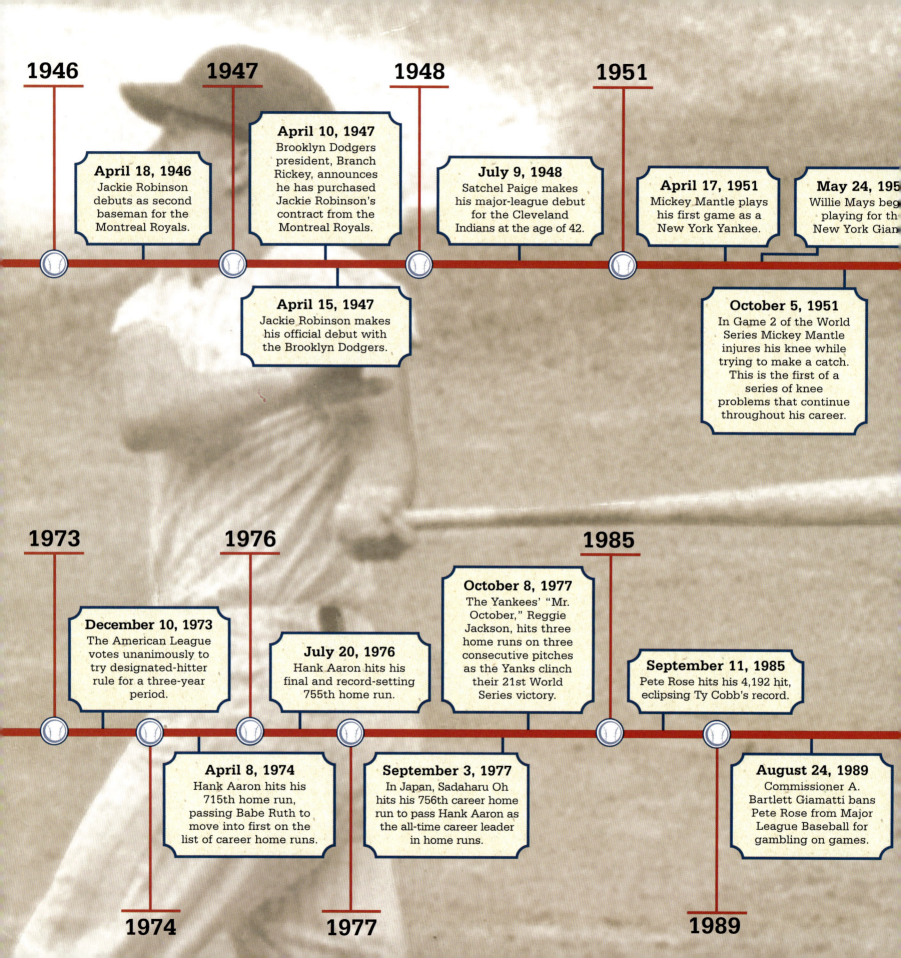

**1946**

**April 18, 1946**
Jackie Robinson debuts as second baseman for the Montreal Royals.

**1947**

**April 10, 1947**
Brooklyn Dodgers president, Branch Rickey, announces he has purchased Jackie Robinson's contract from the Montreal Royals.

**April 15, 1947**
Jackie Robinson makes his official debut with the Brooklyn Dodgers.

**1948**

**July 9, 1948**
Satchel Paige makes his major-league debut for the Cleveland Indians at the age of 42.

**1951**

**April 17, 1951**
Mickey Mantle plays his first game as a New York Yankee.

**May 24, 195[1]**
Willie Mays beg[ins] playing for th[e] New York Gian[ts]

**October 5, 1951**
In Game 2 of the World Series Mickey Mantle injures his knee while trying to make a catch. This is the first of a series of knee problems that continue throughout his career.

**1973**

**December 10, 1973**
The American League votes unanimously to try designated-hitter rule for a three-year period.

**1976**

**July 20, 1976**
Hank Aaron hits his final and record-setting 755th home run.

**April 8, 1974**
Hank Aaron hits his 715th home run, passing Babe Ruth to move into first on the list of career home runs.

**1974**

**October 8, 1977**
The Yankees' "Mr. October," Reggie Jackson, hits three home runs on three consecutive pitches as the Yanks clinch their 21st World Series victory.

**September 3, 1977**
In Japan, Sadaharu Oh hits his 756th career home run to pass Hank Aaron as the all-time career leader in home runs.

**1977**

**1985**

**September 11, 1985**
Pete Rose hits his 4,192 hit, eclipsing Ty Cobb's record.

**August 24, 1989**
Commissioner A. Bartlett Giamatti bans Pete Rose from Major League Baseball for gambling on games.

**1989**